THE MAHELE OF OUR BODIES

THE MAHELE OF OUR BODIES

Nā Moʻolelo Kūpuna Māhū/LGBTQ

Edited by Stephanie Nohelani Teves

University of Hawaiʻi Press
Honolulu

© 2025 University of Hawaiʻi Press
All rights reserved
Printed in the United States of America

First printed, 2025

Library of Congress Cataloging-in-Publication Data

Names: Teves, Stephanie N., editor.
Title: The Mahele of our Bodies : Nā Moʻolelo Kūpuna Māhū /LGBTQ / Stephanie Nohelani Teves.
Description: Honolulu : University of Hawaiʻi Press, [2025] | Includes bibliographical references and index.
Identifiers: LCCN 2024030672 (print) | LCCN 2024030673 (ebook) | ISBN 9780824898496 (hardback) | ISBN 9798880700561 (trade paperback) | ISBN 9798880700585 (epub) | ISBN 9798880700592 (kindle edition) | ISBN 9798880700578 (pdf)
Subjects: LCSH: Sexual minorities—Hawaii. | Sexual minorities—Hawaii—Identity. | Older Hawaiians—Social conditions.
Classification: LCC HQ73.3.U6 T48 2025 (print) | LCC HQ73.3.U6 (ebook) | DDC 306.7609969—dc23/eng/20240823
LC record available at https://lccn.loc.gov/2024030672
LC ebook record available at https://lccn.loc.gov/2024030673

Cover art: "Untitled" painting by Raven O Kaʻapuni, 2023. Courtesy of Keoni Kaʻapuni.

University of Hawaiʻi Press books are printed on acid-free paper and meet the guidelines for permanence and durability of the Council on Library Resources.

Contents

Preface — vii
Acknowledgments — xi

Introduction: The Mahele of Our Bodies — 1

Nā Moʻolelo Kūpuna Māhū/LGBTQ

1. Kuʻumeaaloha Gomes: The Mahele of Our Bodies — 19
2. Noenoe Silva: The Legacies of Nā Mamo — 31
3. Nawahine Dudoit: Coming Home — 39
4. Hōkūokalani Akiu: Learning to Adapt and Survive — 54
5. Kimo Alama Keaulana: If you're nails, I'm the hammer and you're going to get it! — 67
6. Aunty Kim Haʻupu: Resistant Beyond Words — 78
7. Manulani Aluli Meyer: ʻAʻohe pau ke ʻike i ka hālau hoʻokahi — 89
8. Bradford Lum: Becoming a Mentor — 103
9. Lani Kaʻahumanu: Assimilation = Spiritual Erasure — 115
10. Keoni Kaʻapuni: Creating the Self — 132

Epilogue — 146

Bibliography — 149
Index — 151

Preface

The first time I could vote, Hawaiʻi was voting on the issue of same-sex marriage. I went with my parents to the voting location and within the safety of the voting booth, secretly voted "No" against a Hawaiʻi constitutional amendment that would restrict marriage to one man and one woman. Afterwards one of my parents asked how I voted. Terrified, I got up from the dining table and went into my room. I have both vivid and repressed memories of the months leading up to this historic vote in 1998 when advertisements and commercials to "Save Traditional Marriage" were frequent in local media. Members of my family talked about the vote, openly reminding one another to vote "yes" to change Hawaiʻi's constitution to protect heterosexual marriage, as many believed it was under attack by gay people. I was not aware at the time of the historical and political significance of this vote, but I knew that I was gay, Hawaiian, and not "out" to my family. An ongoing feeling of shame permeated most of my life as I did not know any openly gay adults. This made it difficult for me to imagine an adult life for myself, despite the numerous privileges and stability I had grown up with.

I reflect on this moment and am anxious about sharing private details of my life in this way. As an "out" adult in most aspects of my life, I often forget what it is like to live a life where I am afraid at almost every turn that if someone found out intimate details about my life, I could be kicked out of my home, rejected by my family, shunned by community, or lose my job. While getting older has given me the tools to navigate people's perceptions and not care about them, I admit that I am often most anxious within Hawaiian community spaces. I write this from a great space of privilege as a cis woman and as a professor who has still internalized this shame. When I work with college students or other young people, I am reminded that not everyone has gone through this coming out process or is so far along in this journey. I figured it out by learning Hawaiian history, by finding other queers in Hawaiʻi's alternative music and club scenes that became a space of refuge for those of us who dared to buck convention in Hawaiʻi. It is within those spaces that we were able to be our full selves, away from the whispers or judgment of mainstream society. Certainly much has changed since the 1990s when same-sex marriage was a hot button issue in Hawai'i and across the U.S., but there is still so much history to learn about that time. Over the years it became clear to me the need for a Kūpuna Oral History project that centers the voices of Kanaka Maoli Lesbian, Gay, Bisexual, Trans, Queer, Māhū (LGBTQM)[1] people who navigated a modern colonial environment that rewarded heterosexuality and promoted homophobia as common sense.

Teaching on the topic of gender and sexuality at the University of Hawai'i I have observed that there is a knowledge gap amongst young people and society in general. Students are aware that Hawai'i had an early role in the marriage equality debates and many grew up in the early 2010s watching the fight for civil unions and later marriage equality on the news. Many talk about having a Gay-Straight Alliance at their school, openly gay relatives, and even connecting with blatantly queer cartoon characters! Still, their knowledge of queer history was limited to a passing mention of Stonewall, the existence of māhūs, and that AIDS happened at some point long before they were born. With the recent revivial of public anti-gay and especially anti-trans attitudes and legislation, it feels imperative to record the voices of those who lived through prior decades of bigotry and survived. Intergenerational need within the queer community is as urgent as ever, especially as an "out" elderly community grows, as well as remembering those who didn't live to tell their own stories, and to listen to those who are still here.

For these reasons, the Māhū/LGBTQ Kūpuna Oral History project was created as an effort to document and record the experiences of Kānaka Maoli kūpuna (elders) who are also LGBTQM-identified. LGBTQM was framed very loosely when soliciting participants; sometimes it was referred to as the "Gay kūpuna project" or the "LGBTQM kūpuna project." The flexibility of "LGBTQM" was imperative, knowing that Kānaka historically and today have shifting forms of identification that do not always fit within Western LGBTQM identities and politics. Indeed, the majority of kūpuna interviewed in this book described themselves as māhū as well as gay, lesbian, bisexual, or transgender. The primary goal was to talk to kūpuna who were over sixty and who see themselves as both LGBTQM and Kanaka Maoli.

The intentional focus on the Kanaka Maoli or Hawaiian community was necessary to connect with those who had lived during the 1980s and 1990s, when the fight for gay civil rights and same-sex marriage was raging in Hawai'i and across the U.S. At the same time gay civil rights began to emerge in the 1970s, so did the fight for Hawaiian sovereignty. The struggle for Hawaiian sovereignty or

---

1. I include māhū in the popular LGBTQ acronym to acknowledge the varied ways that Kānaka identify.

self-determination dates back to the 1890s, when American businessmen illegally overthrew the Kingdom of Hawai'i. Since then, Kānaka Maoli have labored endlessly to achieve sovereignty, but in the late 1980s and early 1990s, calls for Hawaiian sovereignty were amplified by the centennial anniversary of the overthrow and a mobilization of a number of political groups, including Ka Lāhui Hawai'i, which was the largest and most well known. Several of the interviewees mention Ka Lāhui Hawai'i specifically because of their participation in the group and efforts to have LGBTQM issues included in Ka Lāhui Hawai'i's constitution. The convergence of these two social movements and the experiences of Kanaka Maoli kūpuna have much to teach us about the legacies of colonialism and the challenges kūpuna had to navigate. While Hawai'i is a famously multi-ethnic place with an equally diverse LGBTQM community, Kānaka Maoli people have a unique relationship with history that makes our experiences specific to our identities as both Kānaka and LGBTQM who witnessed Hawai'i's rapid Americanization, alongside growing calls for Hawaiian sovereignty and sexual liberation and openness for non-heterosexual relationships. Both of these congruent issues come up in the interviews, as the speakers discuss how being Kanaka and LGBTQM or just "gay" presented many challenges in their life even as it was a source of strength. I felt it was urgent to focus on the kūpuna who lived through decades of homophobia and bigotry alongside the rise of the sovereignty movement and Hawaiian renaissance.

Finding LGBTQM kūpuna is difficult. It was common to find that many of the well-known LGBTQM kūpuna in the community were no longer living or did not want to talk publicly about this aspect of their lives. I sent many unanswered Facebook messages, emails, and voicemails. This taught me that this demographic was still not comfortable talking publicly about their personal lives (some told me this), despite a few of them being "out" and actually prominent people in the Hawaiian community. It also bears acknowledging that many of the people who lived through this time did not make it to the present, for any number of reasons, thus illustrating the precarity of living a LGBTQM and Hawaiian life.

Recurring themes of shame, silence, marginalization, and, of course, persistence are frequent in the oral histories. Each kupuna shares how their relationship to Hawaiian culture helped to shape their self-acceptance, but that this was always a challenge. There is a perception that the Hawaiian community is very accepting, but many of the interviewees detailed how the Hawaiian community is actually very conservative. This conservativism is related to a suspicion of outsiders, rather than sexuality per se. For example, Hawaiian LGBTQM activists complained about the almost exclusive focus on same-sex marriage in the 1990s within LGBTQM groups that were mainly led by white cis gay men, transplants who knew little about the unique history and social fabric of Hawai'i. Thus, the aversion to outsiders is also a link to the way that LGBTQM issues get framed within the Hawaiian community as a "haole issue" or something to be dealt with after sovereignty. For instance, several kūpuna talked about the homophobia they experienced within the Hawaiian community and how Hawaiian activists were very hesitant to acknowledge sexuality as key to Hawaiian decolonization. This is a struggle that continues today.

In many ways this project was about my own history. As I listened to stories of these kūpuna, it occured to me that I was connected to this history. While I was a teen watching commericals to "Protect Traditional Marriage" that were funded by national conservative political groups, the members of Nā Mamo of Hawai'i were fighting for Kanaka and LGBTQM rights at the legislature. Nā Mamo o Hawai'i was a group of Kanaka and LGBTQM-identified students and staff affiliated with the University of Hawai'i at Mānoa that bridged the university, LGBTQM, and broader Hawaiian community. Their work focused on both Hawaiian sovereignty and LGBTQM issues. Their willingness to be "out" and to fight contributed to the many changes that came to Hawai'i and sociey at large. This project is at once a documentation of the terror of being found out or rejected, but also the glee of finally winning, and watching younger generations unhampered by the same colonial forces that shamed you. So here we are, witness to this moment where the lāhui, understood as a collective of the Hawaiian people who share a common identity and connection, has evolved and returned to these deeper spaces of aloha and pilina (relationships), but never forgetting what it took to get here, knowing that this "here" is precarious, at best.

Acknowledgments

This project would not have been possible without the support of the UH Mānoa Kūaliʻi Council Native Hawaiian Research Support Fund and the Hiʻialo Group at Kamehameha Schools. Additional support was provided by Hui ʻĀina Pilipili; the Department of Women, Gender, and Sexuality Studies; the College of Social Sciences; and the Center for Oral History.

Special mahalo to my patient and diligent research assistants, Sarah Michal Hamid, Kalehuakea Kelling, and Maluhia Low for their immeasurable labor assisting with research, transcription, publicity, and editing. The kōkua of Haʻalilio Solomon and Emma Ching also made this book possible. Finally, my deepest gratitude to the kūpuna in this book who shared their moʻolelo and had faith in the project from the beginning. The lāhui is in your debt. Mahalo nunui.

Introduction
The Mahele of Our Bodies

The "great" mahele in Hawaiian history is a period of time when a capitalist system of land ownership was introduced that transformed the Hawaiian communal ownership of land. The imposition of this system of division forever changed the course of Hawaiian history and the ability for many Kānaka Maoli to live on our ancestral lands. A similar, less talked about mahele also took place, one that happened much more slowly, but was just as devastating. While we became separated from our lands we also became separated from each other through a process of division that solidifed a Euro-American style of family that was different from the extended ʻohana environment that was the norm in Hawaiʻi in the late eighteenth century. New laws impacted how Kānaka Maoli related to one another. A Christian form of "marriage" became institutionalized and other behaviors were deemed indecent and made illegal. This process of changing how Kānaka Maoli related to one another through close physical contact and other forms of intimacy disconnected us from each other's bodies and our own. Kānaka Maoli were expressive people. Our songs, dance, language, games, sport, farming, and other activities all required a kind of embodied knowledge of place, community, rank, family, and other relationships. New words like "adultery," "fornication," "sodomy," "marriage," and other English words transformed our embodied knowledge by prioritizing heterosexual Christian marriage relations as the desired norm, characterizing all other behaviors as illegal, criminal, and sinful.

Kānaka had to be taught that certain behaviors were preferable. These difficult lessons often resulted in arrest or other forms of violence. Over time, we accepted and internalized Christian rules as natural and universal, but this indoctrination was not total. People of course continued to seek out the connections they were accustomed to. Kānaka and incoming immigrants learned quickly that there were consequences for these connections that the new penal codes called adultery, fornication, and a slew of other behaviors the missionaries and the Hawaiian Kingdom sought to stop. While the legal language for such actions intended to code these behaviors as deviant, the words are merely descriptions of the ways that people form connections and relate to one another.

While we might frown upon sexual relations outside of marriage today, it is not against the law. Kānaka did not easily accept the new restrictions, nor did the Chinese, Japanese, Portuguese, Filipinos, or other immigrants who came to work on the plantations and also were subject to these laws and had to learn how to live in the islands under a colonial regime. As the moʻolelo shared in this book reflect, the shifts in Hawaiian relationships had reverberating consequences across the nineteenth and twentieth century.

This book explores the experiences of Kanaka Maoli kūpuna who identify as LGBTQM who lived through many changes in the twentieth century when Hawaiʻi switched from U.S. territory to state, when Hawaiian rights were rising in public consciousness, and the struggle for gay marriage and everything leading up to it transformed Hawaiʻi. Today, the knowledge that our kūpuna continued to have intimate relations with one another despite the missionaries' efforts is a source of inspiration for Kānaka and especially LGBTQM Kānaka today. The voices in these pages carry on this legacy of resistance to heterosexual Christian norms. The moʻolelo shared in this book describe how identifying as "LGBTQ" or "gay" or "māhū" was challenging. Māhū in everyday use in Hawaiʻi often refers to transwomen and effeminate gay men, but broadly can refer to anyone not perceived to be heterosexual, including non-binary, gender fluid, māhū kāne (transmen), lesbians, and many more. It should also be noted that māhū is not necessarily a sexual identity. Māhū was used as a slur for most of the mid- to late twentieth century, but has been reclaimed in recent years. Notably, many of the interviewees in this book referred to themselves as simply "māhū." Identifying in this way divided people from their ʻohana and the lāhui, but they also share how they created different forms of community to push back and make lasting changes so that future generations of Kānaka could express themselves more freely.

Nā Moʻolelo

My first interview was with Kuʻumeaaloha Gomes over the phone. Kuʻumeaaloha was a very public figure in Hawaiʻi in the 1990s. She was prominent in the Hawaiian and LGBTQM community and at the University of Hawaiʻi at Mānoa, where she served as the director of the Kuaʻana Native Hawaiian Student Services center. This is where I first met her in the early 2000s. Kuʻumeaaloha is noted for her role in the film *Ke Kūlana he Māhū* (2000), and she was one of the founders of the group Nā Mamo o Hawaiʻi, who were front and center at the same-sex marriage hearings throughout the 1990s. Because of the group's prominence, Kuʻumeaaloha was asked to serve on the State Commission on Same-Sex Marriage.

It was in this role that she became a public advocate for LGBTQM issues, but as her interview details, she had been involved in political work for many years prior to working on LGBTQM issues. Her oral history alongside several others documents the tensions that arose when non-Hawaiian LGBTQM activists collided with Hawaiian LGBTQM community members who were fighting for both Hawaiian sovereignty and LGBTQM rights. Talking with Kuʻumeaaloha was a critical first step for this project and she was eager to share her insights. She also led me to other Nā Mamo o Hawaiʻi[1] members who were open to talking.

Nawahine Dudoit's contact information was given to me by Kuʻumeaaloha. After I sent her a Facebook message, I learned very quickly that Nawahine, along with most kūpuna, had no problem receiving a phone call from a stranger! This turned out to be a rather consistent method of finding participants for this project. The majority of these kūpuna are active on Facebook and usually within minutes of sending a message, my phone would ring. I met Nawahine in the parking lot of Kalihi Kai Elementary, a school where she used to work. We "talked story" and conducted her interview in her Hyundai Elantra. With Kuʻumeaaloha and Nawahine's connections to Nā Mamo o Hawaiʻi, they led me to other interviewees—Noenoe Silva and Hōkūokalani Akiu. I interviewed both of them in person in the summer of 2021. Hōkūokalani's interview took place at his home in Pālolo. He detailed his life navigating perceptions of what it means to be a Hawaiian man, gay, and surviving as a "working-class" person. Hōkūokalani discussed the tensions he experienced as a member of Ka Lāhui Hawaiʻi, a prominent Hawaiian sovereignty group, and as a gay Hawaiian working toward LGBTQM rights. Noenoe Silva's interview reflects on the legacy of Nā Mamo's political work and what it was like to witness the same-sex marriage legislative hearings that were so homophobic and hateful in nature. Noenoe's reflections provide insight to her life before she became a world-renowned scholar.

Bradford Lum was a student at UH Mānoa during the Hawaiian renaissance in the 1970s, living what he called a "double life." He explained that he had to move to San Francisco to become who he was meant to be. There he got involved with the AIDS activist group ACT UP, which made him feel deeply empowered. This involvement inspired him when he eventually returned to Hawaiʻi and was a key actor in the Marriage Equality movement. Moving to San Francisco or

---

1. Nā Mamo o Hawaiʻi was a LGBTQM political group of community members and people affiliated with the University of Hawaiʻi at Mānoa. Nā Mamo o Mānoa was the original name of the group, focusing on LGBTQM issues, but later the group shifted to being a Kānaka Maoli group focused primarily on the intersections of Hawaiian sovereignty and LGBTQM rights.

visiting there comes up in multiple interviews as a place where observing gay life out in the open made it possible for interviewees to imagine their own lives out of the proverbial closet. Similarly, Keoni Ka'apuni grew up in Hālawa and Makakilo before relocating to New York City and becoming a famous performer known as Raven O. A New York City nightlife fixture for many years, he shared insights about forging one's own path as an artist and how he came to understand himself as māhū. Keoni moved home during the pandemic and had much to reflect on how Hawai'i has changed.

There were many paths taken by the interviewees. Well-known musician and cultural expert Kimo Alama Keaulana is noted for his knowledge of Hawaiian cultural traditions. His interview was conducted over Zoom. In his interview he described what it was like to grow up in a very Hawaiian environment and navigate gay nightlife as a musician and gay Hawaiian man. His interview documents a Honolulu gay club scene in the 1960s and '70s that existed sometimes openly alongside and within "straight" music venues. Kimo's interview is filled with details of a vibrant time in Hawaiian music and performance history. Aunty Kim Ha'upu also reflects on that period of Honolulu nightlife, when the Glade Nightclub and show was a popular spot for the homosexual and "transvestite" māhū community. It was also a place that the vice squad would target, as dressing in a manner not in line with your biological sex was against the law throughout the 1960 and '70s. Aunty Kim shares many tales of her experiences as a māhū, running a business, building community in Wai'anae, and her kuleana to mālama others and future generations.

Manulani Aluli Meyer, an 'Ōiwi philosopher and educator, agreed to talk with me only because I got her name from Ku'umeaaloha. Their interview shares their journey from "jock" to philosopher and how their sexual orientation shaped their lives but was never really the primary way that they publicly presented themselves. The interview was an opportunity to explore how their "orientation," as they described it, impacted the choices they made and how they came to know their role in the Hawaiian community.

The final interview I conducted was with bisexual activist Lani Ka'ahumanu. A Kanaka who has lived away from Hawai'i for the majority of her life, Ka'ahumanu shares her journey from housewife to Grand Marshal of the 1994 San Francisco Pride parade. In her interview, she describes her experiences organizing during the Vietnam War, joining the San Franscisco lesbian community, and then eventually organizing for bisexual recognition within the LGBTQM community. Ka'ahumanu's reflections represent many of the diasporic Kānaka who live on the continent and are often unacknowledged within the Hawaiian LGBTQM community.

From Transcript to Moʻolelo

Each interview was transcribed and then rewritten into a first-person narrative, in the style of what we call in Hawaiian culture, a moʻolelo or story. Moʻolelo can be about the past and project a future; they are often open to interpretation and subject to revision. This is also a form of oral history, oral tradition, or storytelling. This is a dialogic process that honors the participants' input in how their story is told and preserved. While some participants were well known within the Hawaiian community as activists, musicians, or educators, some of them had never talked about their experiences as a "gay Hawaiian," and this project gave them the opportunity to share that part of themselves. At the height of the pandemic in spring 2021, our initial conversations occurred over the phone. The pandemic heightened their awareness of their own vulnerability and served as a reminder of their limited time. I remember telling many of them, *oh the project is no rush*, to which several responded, "*I not going be here forever,*" jokingly. This joke is something we were all very aware of. So, I felt a bit of an urgency but tried not to rush the project.

After each interview was transcribed, the interviewee was sent the transcript for review. Some had no comments, while others had points of clarification or other notes. From there, the transcripts were reworded to reflect a first-person narrative about their life. I went over the transcript with the few who wanted to, but the majority of kūpuna gave me permission to publish their story so that future generations would learn something from it.

While the original intention was to just do audio recordings, several of the kūpuna remarked that it was important for their stories to be part of a book. With their blessing, I moved forward with the project being both for a digital audio archive as well as in printed form. These stories are part of Hawaiian and LGBTQM history and their moʻolelo deserve the material experience of being held in someone's hands.

A History of "Hawaiian Sexuality"

In order to understand and appreciate the experiences of the kūpuna in this book, it is critical to look back at Hawaiian history and consider how ideas of sexuality emerged and changed over time. Sexuality as it is related to behavior or identity is a relatively modern phenomenon. "Sexuality" is a big catch-all term that encompasses a varied history and a range of behaviors. In a given culture or society, people in power aim to manage people's behaviors through laws, social mores, and cultural expectations. In Hawaiʻi, these laws, in the Western sense, did not occur until the early nineteenth century. We must remember that ideas about sexuality are shaped by power, with sex, sexuality, and gender being interwoven. Laws and social norms are mutually constitutive and not static. In other words, they are constantly being challenged and modified.

In this brief history, I have focused on some key points in Hawaiian history that had influence on the lives of the people in this book. Even if the oral history project focuses on people who view themselves as gay, lesbian, bisexual, transgender, or māhū, their lives are connected to the broader community and a number of other issues, such as Hawaiian sovereignty, which was growing in public consciousness at the same time as movements for gay civil rights or liberation. Therefore, to understand the history of sexuality in Hawaiʻi, we need to learn what Kānaka Maoli thought about sexual behavior, how these thoughts and behaviors transformed, who controlled the laws, and what impact the transition from kingdom to fiftieth state had on the sexual practices of people in Hawaiʻi, from all backgrounds.

Kānaka Maoli did not have as many restrictions or labels around sexual behavior as we do today. Translations of Kanaka Maoli epistemology are inadequate in the English language. Still, we can say with confidence that Kānaka Maoli, *i ka wā kahiko*, were sexually fluid. Hawaiian culture has a history of gender fluidity and non-heteronormative sexual practices that can be traced back to antiquity. Numerous accounts in Hawaiian language newspapers affirm this. Descriptions are often found in our moʻolelo that detail the intimate relations of lovers with no gender, of plants and animals that change gender, that reproduce independently, and of partnerships beyond heteromonogamy. Perhaps most famously, the epic tale of Hiʻiakaikapoliopele documents the many travels of Pele and the lovers she acquired.[2] Additionally, aliʻi and akua were known to have numerous aikāne, companions/friends/lovers of the same sex, and there is even a documented instance where one of those lovers was given a formal royal title.[3] These relations

---

2. See Jamaica Heolimeleikalani Osorio, *Remembering Our Intimacies: Moʻolelo, Aloha ʻĀina, and Ea* (Minneapolis: University of Minnesota Press, 2021); Lisa Kahaleole Chang Hall and J. Kēhaulani Kauanui, "Same-Sex Sexuality in Pacific Literature," *Amerasia Journal* 20, no. 1 (1994): 75–82; J. Kēhaulani Kauanui, *Paradoxes of Hawaiian Sovereignty: Land, Sex, and the Colonial Politics of State Nationalism* (Durham, NC: Duke University Press, 2018); Noenoe Silva, "Pele, Hiʻiaka, and Haumea: Women and Power in Two Hawaiian Moʻolelo," *Pacific Studies* 30, no. 1–2 (2007): 159–182; kuʻualoha hoʻomanawanui, *Voices of Fire: Reweaving the Literary Lei of Pele and Hiʻiaka* (Minneapolis: University of Minnesota Press, 2014).
3. See "In the time of Kaomi," in J. Kēhaulani Kauanui, *Paradoxes of Hawaiian Sovereignty: Land, Sex, and the Colonial Politics of State Nationalism* (Durham, NC: Duke University Press, 2018).

and expressions predate and exceed the state, which is why they continue to be such powerful forms of identification for Kānaka Maoli people in the present. Prior to colonization, sexual relations in Hawai'i between people of all genders were permissible among the maka'āinana (commoners). Hawaiian pre-colonial society included an array of sexual practices and coupling arrangements, where what we call polyamory, bigamy, same-sex relationships, and other relationships were common. What might be called "transgender" today was present, usually being referred to as "māhū," which although it is used today to describe a gender identity, there is debate as to whether māhūs were healers, hermaphrodites, or both, but it was not traditionally considered a gender or sexual orientation. So, let's be clear: these identities and practices were not the same as lesbian, gay, transgender, bisexual, or any other "Western" terms that people use currently. We may be inspired by this history and we may think of them as linked, but they are different.

The idea of "Hawaiian sexuality" can be traced to Hawaiian encounters with early missionaries who were invested in controlling Hawaiian sexual behavior. In the late eighteenth and early nineteenth centuries, Euro-American cultures became obsessed with sex. As Michel Foucault has theorized, the management and indexing of sexual acts was part of a larger cultural desire to understand the self in addition to controlling society.[4] This need to control was often motivated by a religious ideology. In a Hawaiian historical context, this means that when sailors and Christian missionaries arrived, they encountered Kānaka Maoli who did not have the same ideas about sexual activity that they did. Armed with Judeo-Christian ideologies, missionaries endeavored to change Hawaiian culture into one deeply informed by Christian morality.

Prior to European contact and influence Kānaka Maoli lived with a relative cultural understanding of customs and protocols related to relationships with the spiritual and physical environment. Intimate relationships among people existed within a structure, often according to political rank and status. There were strict rules around mating for high-ranking people. What we understand to be love or romance existed on a spectrum that included long-term coupling and intimate and platonic friendship, with monogamy being very rare. During the 1820s, Christian missionaries began arriving in the islands and their spiritual and political influence transformed the Hawaiian belief system, demonizing and making illegal many behaviors and practices.

Official printed laws emerged in English only when sailors arrived and began to leave their ships to venture on land. The first recorded laws were instructions

---

4. Michel Foucault, *The History of Sexuality*, ed. Frederic Gros, trans. Robert Hurley, 1st American ed. (New York: Pantheon Books, 1978).

for sailors to stay on their ships at night or not associate with strangers (1822). Known for their drunkenness, associating with Native women, and open defiance of aliʻi, sailors were a common enemy of missionaries and aliʻi alike. Between 1820 and 1840 the population growth of foreigners (sailors, merchants, missionaries) greatly impacted the kānāwai (laws) that were made. Aliʻi had to balance these new foreign interests with the protection of Hawaiʻi and its Native people. Missionaries quickly got into the business of converting Kānaka Maoli and especially convincing nā aliʻi that Christianity was the path to salvation and civilization. The frequent spread of haole-introduced diseases made this conversion argument particularly salient. While many historical accounts have noted the missionary influence, as Noelani Arista explained, understanding the actions of aliʻi at this time is not solely about documenting their acquiesence or resistance, but taking note of the larger context in which new laws were being written.[5] While the specificities of this shifting time in Hawaiian history is beyond the scope of this work, it bears repeating that in the creation of new legal codes, Christian ideals of morality were pervasive. Further, aliʻi were critical in declaring these laws on their own terms, not just because missionaries may have advised them to do so. Aliʻi were highly organized across the archipelago and worked together to design laws they felt were in the best interest of the lāhui at the time.

Kuhina Nui Kaʻahumanu, one of the earliest converts to Christianity, famously decreed an oral penal code forbidding murder, fornication, prostitution, drunkenness, theft, or work on the sabbath (1825). This met opposition from haoles, notably sailors who were known to indulge these behaviors and were quite vocal against the new restrictions on women going on board the ships. Additionally, Kaʻahumanu codified the requirement of marriage for adults engaged in sexual relations. Adults who had been cohabitating were to be considered "married" even if not formally by a priest. Many Kānaka also got married at this time, not realizing the consequences for other behaviors they were used to, such as what the missionaries called "adultery." The laws that were written mirrored those of the New England states from which the missionaries came, Massachusettes in particular. In 1845 marriage in Hawaiʻi rendered Hawaiian women civilly dead, in contrast to the relative freedom and power they exercised prior to missionary arrival. Sodomy was also criminalized in an 1850 legal code that came with a $1,000 fine or twenty years' hard labor. This law would remain on the books in Hawaiʻi well into the twentieth century. A series of other laws constrained women's agency,

---

5. Noelani Arista, *The Kingdom and the Republic: Sovereign Hawaiʻi and the Early United States* (Philadelphia: University of Pennsylvania Press, 2018).

including taking away the right of women to vote and requiring women to take the name of their husband.

Moe Kolohe

In the mid-nineteenth century Kānaka Maoli were over represented in adultery and fornication cases. A decree against "moe kolohe" broadly defined as licentious behaviors like adultery or fornication got many Kānaka in trouble. "Moe kolohe" was an all-encompassing term that the missionaries created because ʻōlelo Hawaiʻi was so specific that Kānaka allegedly continued to engage in many different acts to circumvent the rules around sexual behavior. Moe kolohe operated as a catch-all, based on Christian ideals that worked to redefine marriage and family through the law in Hawaiʻi. Legal ramifications for adultery and fornication were swift and tied to a criminal structure that incentivized policing and prosecution. Police officers and constables were awarded a portion of the fines collected from those found guilty of these behaviors.[6] A culture of surveillance made common people hyper-aware of officials seeking to catch them in the act. With fines often too high to be paid, those found guilty were sent to hard manual labor for a time. Taken together, the legal changes that sought to change Kanaka Maoli attitudes and behaviors around marriage and sexuality were part of a larger civilizing project to make the Hawaiian Kingdom respectable in the eyes of foreigners (and God), which required the building of homes with walls and partitions, the widespread practice of monogamous marriage, the institution of wage labor, and plantation-style farming.

After the overthrow, the Territory period continued many of these penal codes around sexual behavior (adultery, bigamy, etc.). The penalties for such behaviors remained the same. Many arrests and prosecutions for "criminal offenses" like adultery continued to be published in the newspapers, along with divorces. Over the first twenty years within the Territory period, adultery was still being prosecuted as a criminal case, although the numbers decreased dramatically and fornication appears less in the arrest logs. It was said by one Honolulu judge that the cases of adultery were too common to prosecute and that it was happening across all social classes. There were thus calls for adultery to be moved to civil courts and not tried as criminal cases. Adultery and fornication remained in the Hawaiʻi penal code until 1972.

---

6. Sally Engle Merry, *Colonizing Hawaiʻi: The Cultural Power of Law* (Princeton, NJ: Princeton University Press, 2020).

During the early twentieth century, there was a "red light district" in Iwilei on the island of Oʻahu. Prostitution had been mostly legal since the 1860s, as long as the prostitutes registered with the government, were subject to regular health checks, and tested for venereal diseases. It was considered a necessary "social evil" for many years, as plantation worker migration of mostly men increased and later during World War II the presence of American servicemen ballooned. In 1930 prostitution was made illegal, but was quietly tolerated by the public because it was highly regulated by the local police. A "vice district" in what is today Honolulu's Chinatown is where numerous prostitution houses operated under the surveillance of local police and business owners who were all on the take. Not surprisingly this lucrative industry became an efficient machine during wartime when it is estimated a million servicemen came to Pearl Harbor and two hundred prostitutes had to serve all of them. There were plenty of opportunities for soldier rest and relaxation while on island. An entire side economy was attached to prostitution that created a carnival-like atmostphere in Chinatown. Sailors often posed with hula girls, got tattoos, got drunk, gambled, and paid for sex all in the same block. Honolulu's Hotel Street became notorious at this time and continues to be known as the place where soldiers went for "three dollars for three minutes" sex and other general amusement. The U.S. military was actively invested in maintaining the system of brothels in some ways as a matter of national security. There was much tension between the military, the police, and the prostitutes at this time concerning the rights of the prostitutes, as well as disputes over the access and cost of the services. From 1941 to 1943 prostitution was a necessary part of wartime life and many residents felt it alleviated many of the stresses of martial law and provided an outlet for the hordes of servicemen that most importantly kept them from acting out or against the local community, especially towards local women.[7] However, shortly after martial law ended, an antiprostitution movement grew, claiming that such behaviors were negative for society and set a poor moral standard for children. Prostitution became outlawed again in 1945 and went underground.

By the time Hawaiʻi became a state in 1959, many of the penal codes relating to adultery, marriage, and fornication were dealt with as civil rather than criminal legal matters. Growing McCarthyism and the Cold War pegged communists and homosexuals as threats to American life, known as the "Lavender Scare," which was also present in Hawaiʻi. At the same time, discussions of sex from a

---

7. Beth Bailey and David Farber, *The First Strange Place: The Alchemy of Race and Sex in World War II Hawaii* (New York: Free Press, 1992).

psychological and anthropological perspective became popular. The work of sexologist Dr. Alfred Kinsey showed that most people had homosexual or bisexual desires, despite public aversion to such behaviors. Not surprsingly, this was coupled with growing local interest in solving the problem of homosexuality as a social ill or mental disorder. In the 1960s there were a series of newspaper articles describing the activities of gay bars in Honolulu and how Hawai'i had become a destination for gay travelers, usually from the West Coast. The military of course was also concerned about homosexuality in its ranks and how servicemembers spent their time on-island. Military personnel were banned from many of these establishments, although they still frequented them. Kimo Alama Keaulana, one of the kūpuna who shared their stories in this book, details how there was an elaborate maze of back alleys in Chinatown where military personnel would escape when the military police came to raid the bars. The vice squad and military police kept records on known homosexuals and would go undercover to pick up/arrest people for engaging in homosexual activity. Referred to as homosexuals, transvestites, and transsexuals, they were targeted in vice raids and new legislation. The Mayor's Committee on Children and Youth created a Subcommittee on Sexual Deviants that partnered with the police and aligned itself with medical officials and churches to push a new law that would declare "masquerading as a female" a misdemeanor. In 1963, Act 175, the "intent to deceive" or "dressing to deceive" law was passed as a way to mitigate growing homosexual activity.[8] The Glade Nightclub, a popular Chinatown club on Hotel Street, was a deliberate target of this legislation. The Glade especially was known for its female impersonation dinner shows. It was a popular hot spot for tourists, locals, and military personnel alike. The performers, many who were men that either performed as women or lived as women on and off the stage, had to wear buttons that said "I am a boy" so that patrons knew the "biological sex" of the person they were with. This was required of all people who did not dress in the manner of their biological sex.[9] The Glade is perhaps the most remembered club today, but there was also The Clouds, Market Cafe, The Roosevelt Cocktail Lounge, and The Apartment, which was a private gay club strictly off-limits to female impersonators. Interviews with māhū or homosexuals at this time illustrate that there was a differentiation within the community among "homosexuals" as those who are discreet and live normal lives (i.e., married w/kids) despite their desires and those who are overt and dress as the other sex.

8. Bob Jones, "Action Is Sought on Isle Deviants," *Honolulu Advertiser*, February 14, 1963.
9. Wes Young, "World of the Homosexual," *Honolulu Star-Bulletin*, February 29, 1964.

"Māhūs No Make Trouble"

Throughout the 1960s, homosexuals were still considered "deviant" and ostracized, but there was some murmur within the local gay community of seeking human rights, being "born this way," contributing to society, and even what would later be called same-sex marriage. A 1968 news story, "Mahu Are People, Too," detailed the process of a gay marriage between two men and how such unions were entered into.[10] Gay bars in Waikīkī and Chinatown are well-known within the local community and young people are noted for hanging around these areas, much to the concern of parents. Bars cater to tourists, military, locals, and anyone "curious" as it was described in a 1967 exposé on the growing homosexual community in Hawai'i.[11] Business owners say that māhūs are good costumers and don't cause trouble.

With the growth of a local gay community and changing sexual behaviors within society at large, social expectations around gender, sexuality, and marriage began to shift. Feminism had a huge impact on this environment of "free love" and expanded rights for women in Hawai'i, which were believed to be some of the most progressive in the US. Hawai'i was the first state to ratify the Equal Rights Amendment in 1972 and an early adopter of abortion rights in 1970. By the 1970s, the local gay and lesbian community began to publish newsletters, hold more public events, and become less closeted. Relaxed attitudes toward sexual behavior and increased awareness of privacy rights ushered in changes to the Hawai'i criminal code in 1973, which eliminated "sex laws" like adultery, fornication, and sodomy as criminal offenses, which were to be treated instead as private matters between consenting adults. Prostitution became a petty misdemeanor. The "intent to deceive" act was also removed. In 1978 Hawai'i added to its Bill of Rights the "right to privacy" to the extent that the state could provide a "compelling state interest" against it. This "compelling state interest" would later become a wedge in the state's desire to ban gay marriage in the 1990s.

The first case of HIV was identified in Hawai'i in 1983. By June 1986 there were 100 AIDS cases reported in Hawai'i and that number continued to double annually. By the early 1990s there were over 800 AIDS cases in Hawai'i, the majority being adults, notably among gay and bisexual men. During the early years of the epidemic, gay white men made up the majority of cases, but through prevention and education, the cases went down.

---

10. Melvin Goo, "'Mahus Are People, Too—Hawaii's Loneliest Citizens," *Honolulu Advertiser*, July 17, 1968.
11. Gene Hunter, "No Signs Point Way to 'Hangouts,'" *Honolulu Advertiser*, September 25, 1967.

Unfortunately, prevention measures were not as well known within the Asian and particularly the Pacific Islander community, which saw AIDS positivity rates increase throughout the early 1990s, in addition to the growing number of heterosexuals and women in particular who contracted the disease from their closeted male partners, sex work, or intravenous drug use. By the late '90s there were estimated between 3,000 and 6,000 HIV-positive individuals who were living with AIDS. Hawaiʻi believed itself to be a leader in the fight, opening the first federally funded HIV antibody testing site in 1985, which offered free and anonymous testing, as well as one of the a few states that allowed Medicaid participants to receive homecare services. The Hawaiʻi public school system had a robust education program in 1987, one of the earliest states to do so.

On the surface Hawaiʻi seemed to be a leader on AIDS prevention, but there was still a lot of fear and homophobic conservative beliefs that pervaded politics in the 1980s. As time went on, more human interest stories showcased "normal" local people who were living with AIDS in the shadows. A topic seldom discussed within the Hawaiian community, AIDS could no longer be ignored by the mid-1990s as a number of prominent kumu hula and others within the hula community were dying of AIDS.[12] As discussed in Hōkūokalani Akiu's interview, many hālau were feeling the impact of AIDS and some kumu even forbid dancers from going to gay bars or being out in hālau. This reality was felt throughout the Hawaiian community as public awareness of the impact of the epidemic grew. Bradford Lum, Keoni Kaʻapuni, and Lani Kaʻahumanu discuss in their interviews what it was like to get involved with AIDS activism on the continent and how they were part of the struggle to fight for the health care and medicines that eventually became available after years of government denial.

Compelling State Interest

The 1990s was a vibrant time for LGBTQM issues and the Hawaiian sovereignty movement. Three same-sex couples famously applied for marriage licenses from the Hawaiʻi Department of Health on December 17, 1990. The applicants were denied marriage licenses, resulting in a lawsuit against the State of Hawaiʻi on the basis of sex discrimination, claiming that the plantiffs' privacy and equal protection rights on the basis of sex were violated, which the Hawaiʻi Supreme Court in 1996 later affirmed. While the state tried to argue that it had a "compelling state interest" to prevent same-sex marriage, because of the possible impact

---

12. Advertiser Staff, "Kumu Hula, AIDS Activist Kahala Dies," *Honolulu Star Bulletin*, November 5, 1991.

on tourism or the family (i.e., children), they were unable to demostrate that same-sex marriage would dramatically impact either. The ruling sent political shockwaves across the U.S., spreading the perception that same-sex marriage was legal in Hawaiʻi. Challenges in other states were imminent, inspiring President Bill Clinton's Defense of Marriage Act (DOMA) in 1996.

Hōkūokalani Akiu and Noenoe Silva were both active in the Hawaiian LGBTQM activist group Nā Mamo o Hawaiʻi. What was remarkable about Nā Mamo was their explicit committment to Hawaiian sovereignty. In the early 1990s Hawaiian sovereignty intensified in public discourse as calls for some form of Hawaiian independence grew out of the centennial anniversary of the illegal overthrow of the Hawaiian Kingdom and the adoption of the "Apology Resolution" in 1993 by the U.S. Congress that apologized for the United States' role in the illegal overthrow of the Hawaiian Kingdom. It was at the centennial march that Haunani-Kay Trask defiantly proclaimed on the steps of the Kapiʻolani Park Bandstand, "We are Not American!" As Nawahine Dudoit describes in her interview, coming home to Hawaiʻi and being at the January 17, 1993, centennial march and hearing Trask give this historic speech greatly inspired her as a Hawaiian and, later, as a māhū fighting for LGBTQM rights.

The question of same-sex marriage was eventually put to a public vote on a constitutuional amendment, which codified marriage between a man and woman in Hawaiʻi. This ostensibly banned same-sex marriage in 1998. While the question of same-sex marriage quietly slipped out of mainstream media discourse in Hawaiʻi, it had already shored up much of the shame around non-normative sexuality that existed within the Hawaiian community. It also shone a spotlight on the question of Hawaiʻi's economic engine, tourism, and what role it would have in determining Hawaiʻi's economic priorities, as the specter of gay marriage emerged in the popular discourse about Hawaiʻi. Notably this discourse drew on the fantasy of the Pacific as space of sexual freedom, despite the role colonialism played in the suppression of sexual expression in the islands.

By the early 2000s, same-sex marriage legal challenges swept across the U.S. Interestingly at this time in Hawaiʻi, there is a rise in business and state support of gay tourism in the islands as the power of the "Pink Dollar" appealled to lawmakers and business owners eying the "mainland" gay community as an untapped market. As same-sex marriage was legalized in many U.S. states, the activists involved in Nā Mamo went about their lives and continued the work they were doing in the Hawaiian community. Several remarked feeling burnt out, deeply disappointed by the racism within the LGBTQM community and the homophobia within the Hawaiian community. On a larger scale, public opinion about same-sex marriage began to shift, now under the moniker of "marriage equality" and was growing in support. Civil unions passed the Hawai'i Senate in 2011. The growing support for LGBTQM rights was palpable at the hearings, which built momentum for 2013's eventual passing of marriage equality. After 55 hours of public testimony, then Hawai'i governor Neil Abercrombie signed into law the Hawai'i Marriage Equality Act of 2013. Many people felt this was a full circle moment, as Hawai'i was the first state to legally consider same-sex marriage in the landmark 1991 case *Baehr v. Lewin*, which started a tidal wave of political and legal implications for same-sex marriage across the U.S. Some of the leading activists did not live to see that day, while others who had given so much during their own time watched with joy as a new generation of activists achieved this landmark moment.

Don't Say Gay

The moʻolelo of the kūpuna in this book document their experiences amidst the rapid transformation of LGBTQM public life. They fought for historic legal changes and cultural shifts that made LGBTQM people more open and accepted. They witnessed the rise of rainbow capitalism and representational politics that feature openly queer people in news, television, movies, advertising, and government. In the early 2020s, however, new legislative efforts such as "Don't say gay" bills advanced in a number of U.S. states, aiming to "empower parents" and police the teaching of LGBTQM topics in schools, in addition to creating new restrictions on gender-affirming care for adolescents (and adults in some states), and an overregulation of drag performance in public and even private spaces. While these efforts have been emerging in Hawai'i, legislation has not gained much traction, yet. Still, opposition to LGBTQM rights is growing along with other forms of misinformation on social media. This has put the LGBTQM community in a renewed state of insecurity, and young people in particular have voiced their fears, expressing their anxieties about how they will navigate (and survive) this changing landscape.

The kūpuna in this book have much to teach us about how they survived. Their voices complicate the histories of LGBTQM acceptence in broader society and within the Hawaiian community. It is now our collective kuleana (responsibility) to learn this history and listen to the voices of the kūpuna who lived it.

Nā Moʻolelo Kūpuna Māhū/LGBTQ

Kuʻumeaaloha Gomes
The Mahele of Our Bodies

In the Mahele people had to register their land, so doing that is like being put in boxes. It sets you apart from other people, those who have those, who don't have. You create fences. Not everybody could do that, not everybody could read, not everybody could go to where the official said you had to go to register stuff. They put up barriers, the same way with our bodies. Our bodies are not meant to be put in chains, our bodies are not meant to be restricted. Our bodies are meant for us to be very expressive. Hawaiians were like that. We were intelligent people. We did not wear clothes because it was hot. We didn't need to. We were later told to cover up because the missionaries were afraid of looking at us and heaven forbid we see each other's bodies. To me it was an expression of the mahele of our bodies, the restriction of our bodies, the control of our expression of our bodies. Whereas before we didn't have that ownership, now because of Western concepts that are based on economy and ownership, all of a sudden we're restricted in the way we express ourselves and allow our bodies to be.

When I was born at St. Francis Medical center, my father called my Hawaiian tūtūlady (grandmother), and told her "Malia gave us a baby girl" and she told him, her name will be "Kuʻumeaaloha." My Tūtū had a dream about me and the name came to her. She knew that the name would be a lot to carry, but that I would use this name to overcome different struggles and obstacles in life, but that those experiences would give me the wisdom to forgive people and share aloha throughout my life.

My tūtū was a lāʻau lapaʻau and hoʻoponopono practitioner, which I am now. She knew this name would fit me and it turns out it has through all the things I have gone through and the manaʻo I have to share about forgiveness and aloha. When I was little my Tūtū would teach me about lāʻau lapaʻau medicines so I could help my cousins and friends. When my parents divorced, my Tūtū reminded me not to hold things against people. She taught me about Papa and Wākea, who were the earth and sky, who birth all of Hawaiian creation, including my parents.

She taught me to have aloha for these things because they take care of you, even when they disappoint you or hurt you, you must always care for them. The emphasis on healing and understanding was taught to me since birth and has carried into every aspect of my life.

When I was young my family moved to Kekaha, Kauaʻi, and we lived on a sugar plantation where my father was a machinist. My grandpa was the luna at the plantation camp. My dad had to deal with lots of issues from the workers and this taught me about working-class struggle. My uncle would take me around to all the different sections of the camps when he pau hana. We went to the Filipino camp and we would watch the fighting chickens, in the Japanese camp they would often give me fruits, and in the Hawaiian camp, I would sometimes watch the kids.

I once did a group project to help my dad's employees get a raise. My dad became a contractor building industrial fences and he hired many different kinds of workers. He would hire older Filipino men who retired from the plantations or men that just got out of prison. They were really grateful for the work. I went around without my father's knowledge and interviewed many of them and calculated why they deserved a raise. When I showed my dad, he was proud, even though he may not have liked the outcome, he liked that I took the initiative. My dad, I think later, felt this way even though I never came out to him, he was proud that I was asked to be on the State Commission on Same-Sex Marriage. He felt proud that I could be on that level. He was especially proud because I was involved as a commissioner with his friend Tom Gill.

After my parents divorced, my father married another woman on Oʻahu who was not very kind to me and she favored her own children over me and my siblings. She would give us girls less lunch money than her sons. I attended public school and it was hard for Polynesians, the teachers did not expect much academically from Hawaiians. We were stereotyped as low-performing intellectually. I remember having my first crush on a girl in the fifth grade and I would carry her books. I remember seeing some kids later that were girl-girl and liking that, but I knew that was not what we were supposed to do.

After high school, I did the LPN (licensed practical nurse) program at KCC (Kapiʻolani Community College). I got married, had a son, and got divorced. I moved to Kauaʻi, where I began working in community mental health. I helped develop the first halfway house for challenged teens and I worked with the local police to develop domestic violence response teams. I worked at the Samuel Mahelona hospital as a nurse with kūpuna and learned really how alone they can be. I would just climb into bed and hold them. After that, I moved back to Oʻahu and started working at Waiʻanae Mental Health Center giving parenting classes at the Lualualei military installation. When I was teaching the class, I could feel something was off, like there was something blocking my connection with the women. So, I just asked, and finally the women confessed that they were told not to trust me! They had been told that all Hawaiians hate them (the military). This was at the time of PKO (Protect Kahoʻolawe ʻOhana) and RIMPAC, so there was lots of criticism of the military in Hawaiian communities, but I explained to them why, and the history and everything, so that they understand it was not personal. They were really impacted by it and crying, but before I knew it, this woman stood up in the back of the room and started saying that she was waiting for me to bring like, Hawaiian politics up, and before I knew it, I was being quickly escorted off base. I was scared I was going to lose my job! When I got back to work, my boss came after me, but the UPW union agent told me no worry because I was protected. Then, Pōkā Laenui Burgess joked that I had made some special list of activist Kānaka who cannot go onto base. That kind of propelled me into PKO, I had people calling me up saying "congratulations" and "come join us" you know that kind of stuff.

Coming Out

I tried getting married in a heterosexual marriage, but it did not work because I was always thinking of females and it was very confusing. There was no community here that I was attached to. During the Nuclear Free and Independent Pacific Movement in 1986, I went to Aotearoa for the Waitangi march, I represented Hawaiʻi with all these other activists. They had me staying with these women and I did not even know they were all gay. I ended up getting the flu and they all took care of me. These two women, one on each side of me, they took care of me, combing my hair and massaged me and just so loving. I felt something break inside of me, I imagined it like chains that had kept me from really expressing myself. I felt myself break open. I felt this tremendous love from these other women and they began to talk to me about it, they said, "We know that you're a lesbian like us, you're a dyke," and they used that word. They said, "We know that you're a dyke like us, it's just that you haven't been expressing it." Nobody was trying to get with me or anything, they were just expressing all this love and taking care of me. They had this amazing community of women there, not just of dykes, but of women who supported each other. I observed how the women organized around someone experiencing spouse abuse. After the march, one of the heterosexual women invited us to stay at her farm. We got word that one of the women who had two children had gotten beaten by her husband. They quickly organized a group of women to support the victim and they took over her house, kicked the guy out and gathered the husbands to hold him accountable. The women massaged this woman back to health, took care of her family, everything just so she could heal. They even protested outside of the husband's work to encourage the boss to hold him accountable for his behavior. I thought, we need this in Hawai'i! One time, I was involved in the PKO Women's group and Haunani-Kay Trask, Miliani Trask, Marion Kelly, and others, I shared with them what I observed and Haunani got really excited by it, she says, "We need to name ourselves Wāhine Koa! We need to be the women warriors and we need to do this!" and it unfortunately happened later within the larger group. I brought all of that back from the Aotearoa experience.

It wasn't until I went to UCSF that I met many women in 1990. I was in San Francisco for about a year and a half in a program for minorities in research careers. Of course in San Francisco you get involved and I started to look and listen and observe and it felt good. There was a difference between the two communities. In Aotearoa, it was more conservative there in terms of women with women in traditional homosexual relationships, like not having multiple partners like I saw in San Francisco. It was very creative in San Francisco, a woman could be married to a man and have a female partner as long as she didn't do it in front of her husband. There were people who had S&M relationships, it was very different than in Aotearoa. I was exposed to this, so when I came home it was like, yeah it's time to come out. I could no longer remain in the closet, be oppressed, and not express myself. I grew up in a very Catholic family, we had two nuns and a priest in the family! The Catholic upbringing restricted me from being around people who were gay.

Having the Aotearoa and San Francisco experience, it helped me to set a standard for myself because I couldn't express myself as a "dyke" like the Māori, Aotearoa people or flexible relationships in San Francisco, but I had to be me and set my standards and I knew I had to take an activist role and to be a role model too. I thought about what it means to be able to talk to my peers and to people that I was going to mentor without being judgmental because that's what I grew up with. How do we allow people to be and yet be proud of themselves and who they are and not accept lower standards. I would see gay relationships that are like heterosexual relationships, you can have abuse. Don't glorify it, it's not a perfect relationship, there are issues too and we need to talk about it.

When I came home after that, that was when I started expressing myself more, as Hawaiian and gay and there was no stopping after that. Because of PKO, I came home and started calling myself a lesbian. People in the group would ask me why I started using that word and I had to come out and tell them that's who I am, I am a lesbian. In Hawai'i we would say "gay woman" so I would say that, we did not say lesbian, we said "gay men and women." People questioned me about it. I started reaching out to different women, but the white women in the community didn't resonate with me. As a woman of color, I was looking for women like me. There were some Asian women that I met, other women were more butchy women, you know Hawaiian butchy women, but I am not a butchy type, so I was kind of scared and distant and just watched them and it's like, I did not want to get too close, they were too aggressive for me. There was a place on University called "the women's coffee shop" and it was in the YWCA building. It had events where women gathered. They had musicians and poetry nights, that's where I met a lot of women of color who were gay, was at the women's coffee shop. For women of color this was mostly their safe space, so it was maintained for a long time. It was from there that I met a lot of other women of color, but they weren't involved in organizing. They tended not to do that, they were more in private, in relationships, in communities living together, happy, a little shyer, more private. I remember I would be talking about politics and they would tease me that I was kind of out there. They would tell me, "Kuʻumeaaloha, leave us alone!" because I was always talking politics.

In a Hawaiian sense I always had a hard time with the lesbian thing, just being lesbian. Hawaiian sexuality is expressed on a spectrum, we are not meant to be in boxes with the labels, it's really a Western concept to set people apart. I always had a difficult time with the same-sex marriage project because of the labels that they used and the failure to recognize that this was Hawaiʻi and Hawaiian culture expresses sexuality in a different way. The gay movement was trying to make Hawaiians fit into their boxes and we didn't fit. At first I saw myself as a lesbian in those other places, but later I saw myself expanding. I could do whatever I wanted to do, I was not meant to be in a box. I had to take all those walls down and just express myself on a very broad spectrum to have the freedom to do that for my soul, so my soul could be happy. That feeds my soul and naʻau. What makes me comfortable in who I am and our sexuality was expressed on a spectrum. Our people always looked to nature for their answers. They got the design for kapa from plants. Cutting a stem and there's design in the stem. You look at the leaves and shapes of leaves and then I began to look at sexuality in the same way. Looking to nature is like looking at how plants are mating, you see when a seed germinates with another seed. That is how my mind works, seeing things and learning not always from books, but looking to nature where there are expressions. Then eventually we formed Nā Mamo o Hawaiʻi. We formed it to have a voice for gay people within the sovereignty movement and at the same time, for the same-sex marriage hearings. We suddenly became very visible and verbal in the community.

Nā Mamo o Hawaiʻi, 1995. First row: Kuʻumeaaloha Gomes, Alison Artie; Second row: Monoʻiki AhNee-Bahn, Cameron Miyamoto, Noenoe Silva; Third row: Nawahine Dudoit, Ann Sturgis, Kelaiki Keala. Courtesy of Kuʻumeaaloha Gomes.

Nā Mamo o Hawaiʻi

I observed lots of organizing in San Francisco and I knew it had to be done in Hawaiʻi and felt it was my place to do it. This related to my childhood because it was all part of confronting the need for peace and justice. It was easy for me to talk to people and to help bring our voices together. Amy Agbayani, who was my supervisor at the University of Hawaiʻi and friend of Governor Cayetano, suggested to him to have me on the Commission on Same-Sex Marriage and the Law. The chairperson was Tom Gill, little did I know he was actually friends with my dad when I was little. So my dad, remember I said he was proud of me even though I never came out, he was proud to see his daughter work with somebody he had a lot of respect for.

During the hearings it was very hard listening to all the bigoted comments, but what made it bearable was seeing Nā Mamo people sitting in the front, the two front rows. They would sit there and shake their heads or sometimes smile at me. There were times you want to burst out, but you of course cannot do it, you have to let people talk. The Nā Mamo folks committed themselves to coming out and they did. They had courage and it was just amazing. Same thing in the sovereignty movement. People like Kekuni Blaisdell, Aʻo Pōhaku, Bumpy Kanahele, they really welcomed the gay community into the sovereignty movement. They understood that it wasn't an issue, we just wanted to sit at the table too. There was pushback in both the Hawaiian community and the gay white community. Not that we wanted to raise our issues, it's just that we wanted it to be recognized in our community that we have homophobia and if we are going to form a nation, we cannot replicate that. We got a lot of support from Hawaiian women whose husbands were leaders in the sovereignty movement, they were happy that we were speaking out and they shared with us that spouse abuse was a really big issue too. They talked about their husbands and child abuse too.

Of course the men leaders denied this was an issue, they wanted to sweep this under the carpet. Our response to this was the ʻAe Like decision-making process, which we worked on for a whole year and then took it to the Pūwalu to all the different communities. We wanted buy-in from everybody. The kūpuna were really into it, in fact, they gave us the name. It was really interesting because we started hearing from all kinds of people like fishermen who were surprised that they could talk at meetings, people felt like they could speak up, because before they thought only attorneys or people from the University could talk. The kūpuna supported us, they say "those gay people they so good, those gay people they bring this stuff so everybody can talk" and it was so funny because at first people talked about us like we were from a different planet, "it's the gay people, it's the gay people!"

People became very open with us, they would share about their grandkids or somebody they knew who was māhū and stuff like that. It became an opportunity to speak freely and they saw us not just as people who were creative or played music, but as smart people who were lawyers, professors, whatever. The ʻAe Like continues to be used today.

The Commission on LGBT Rights & Committee on Same-Sex Marriage

I wanted to be on the commission because I knew people who are involved in policy making can make a difference. I wanted to give voice to those people who aren't given a seat at the table, who cannot speak for themselves. That was the other thing too, in society often times it's those with privilege who speak for others. But, they neva ask! We make the policies and the rules for those who are the most affected, yet they're not at the table to speak for themselves. We see them as victims, yet we don't allow them to express their power. In fact we render them powerless by continuing to keep them as victims.

I felt like a fish out of water on the commission. Some of those people were way more experienced than I was because I come out of the community. Some of those people were directors, politicians, and they came out of that professional setting. I came out of the Hawaiian and gay community. It was difficult often times for me to keep up with them in discussions. I was trying to balance what we were doing and what works and it was hard for me to know my value and how or when I can contribute. I come from that perspective of always making sure that people have voice and visibility and that their stories are validated. That's the place that I come from. Sitting at the table talking policies was new for me. I didn't know if I wanted to be in that arena. The other thing was horrific, was listening to all the testimony. Just sitting through the testimony from the far right made me feel like I was getting punched over and over again and you couldn't do anything. It was so hard. The horrendous things that they were saying, it made me ask, "Who is their Jesus? That's not my Jesus!" My Jesus is compassionate and loving and he cares. My Jesus would not use words like this or say, "These people are an abomination to society and to the human race." It was really hurtful. I would ask, "Who are you talking about?!" They were talking about me and my community and there were times I just had to put my head down and ask where they get this from? There was a theme, it was like they were from a different world, the language they spoke. They came out of the churches and they were captive audiences, so this was their language over and over again. They were bussed in by the busloads. Their only purpose was to take up space and to testify and get on record and say these horrible things about other human beings that they know nothing about. That was the really really hard part.

I remember at one point, I asked myself, how do I not carry this animosity for these people? What can I do so that I can see past the rhetoric and see them as humans who are also victims of their own captivity in organized religion? I went up to Mike Gabbard one time, he was their leader, he was very vocal. He was there all the time at the legislature and he would speak at the hearings all the time. I would watch him and listen to him talk, so one day I got up and I went to him and said, "Mike, you know who I am. And I know who you are. And I just want to tell you that I don't hate you. I admire you." He looked at me, floored. I said, "What I admire is the commitment you make to what you believe and how you stand by that. I may not agree, but I admire your leadership and I wanted you to know that." And I could just see him melt. He went from this you're going to fight with me face to just melting. After that whenever he saw me, he could come up and talk to me very respectfully and very quietly and not have that facade of fighting. He never used that rhetoric with me. I learned from it and it gave me courage and insight. I was honored to work with the other people on the committee who weren't even gay, but who were working for the betterment of the community in Hawai'i.

Along with Nā Mamo, other community groups like the UH LGBT Center came, but Nā Mamo was the most consistent. They always came early, Nawahine Dudoit, Kealaiki Keala, Monoiki Ah Nee, Kalei Puha, Peter Silva, James Mould, Noenoe Silva, those guys always consistent. If they didn't come, they would send a text telling me why and saying their heart was with me.

There were tensions with the white community. The people of color gay community was very separate. The white gay community visibility was mostly gay white men. The people of color one was diverse, you had māhū, you had gay women, you had gay men, it was a very diverse community. The white gay women community was very professional and more closeted. Within the gay community, the white men had boards and positions, management and it was all white, it felt like they did not want people of color to have voice. We had to fight against that, reminding them that this was Hawai'i and that they could not have a monopoly. Around the same-sex marriage issue, the Human Rights Commission came over to help with the same-sex marriage issue and they always talked about civil rights, talking about the struggle going back to Stonewall. We were not from Stonewall and in Hawai'i, we have been expressing our sexuality and our aikāne relationships further than you know! We wanted them to see our expressions also as valid and incorporate it into what we were talking about. They didn't want to do that, they did not want to do that at all and still today, they think this way. They want to talk about aikāne relationships and do hula and be part of Hawaiian music, but not have a deep understanding of Hawaiian culture. In Hawaiian we have the expression "moe aku moe mai," which is an expression of our culture and the broad acceptance of sexuality on the spectrum. They do not get that. There is tremendous value in that which gets silenced. We were being forced again to fit into this box that their policymakers could relate to, to fit this larger picture of what they saw. The gay white transplant community, they don't understand why we are so grounded in this place or how we feel as being part of the 'āina, we are part of it. It's not part of us, we are part of it. They don't understand because they don't have that.

When we had the public debate on TV with Jackie Young and Mike Gabbard, it was really hard because nobody was helping to prep me. I was totally on my own. I was alone as the Hawaiian voice. The Human Rights Commission was prepping Jackie, but nobody prepped me. I was totally on my own and I had to figure out how to do this. In Nā Mamo o Hawai'i I was the most progressive person and I had the training and I was bringing alone the others, so no one could really help me strategize. It was really challenging. If I had known better I would have reached out to friends in Aotearoa or some of my people of color friends in San Francisco to help me strategize. I felt like I was fighting to have a position to have a Hawaiian voice in the debate, trying to push, this is Hawai'i. We had to do that all the way through. I remember feeling that I wanted to give up. It was taking a lot out of me and draining my mana, not being refilling. I would walk around sometimes feeling betrayed by your own gay community. Not the Hawaiian part, but the general part and feel like I let people down because I wasn't good enough or forceful. It felt like being victimized all over again but in a different way.

Hawaiians were very supportive of me, but some were not as helpful. Some criticized me after the debate about how I could have done better, but no one prepped me! It was very difficult, I did not know all the political rhetoric and the debate format. I wish someone helped me have practice sessions. I found myself in a lot of those situations feeling inadequate and not performing as good as I could or should have.

One thing that was extra heartbreaking during this time was seeing all of the Hawai'i Revised Statutes that related to Hawaiian Homelands and how it required you to be heterosexual to inherit your land from your partner. You couldn't be gay. People could be together for years, like my Aunty Lei and my Aunty Mackie, together for fifty years. One of them died and they had Hawaiian Homelands, one of them died and the other couldn't stay there legally. Gay people were like nothing, we had no rights. We are citizens, we are paying taxes and we had no rights. I would ask myself, how can we live in a society like that?

Those kinds of discussions we did not have enough because people kept it on a policy level and we needed to bring it down to this lower level, a community level where I felt more comfortable. I had a hard time talking to the policy people. In Nā Mamo I could talk like that, on a level that everybody felt empowered because they could understand. When I told them about the Hawai'i Revised Statutes and what it said, somebody would cry, it was like, wow, that could be me, that kind of stuff. They understand it at that level. But all this mainland rhetoric and policy rhetoric that's not where our community or people of color community was at.

After the Vote

What happened for me, I was in a nineteen-year relationship and in 2006 my partner passed away. It was before same-sex marriage passed in Massachusetts. On a personal level it was really hard for me. We fought for that, but I couldn't take advantage of it. I had to go through healing after that and it was really hard. I remember at the funeral, Amy (Agbayani) came up to me and said, "I just want you to know that even though she's not here when the law for same-sex marriage gets passed, and it is getting passed, in the eyes of God, you are married," it was a real victory and a nice celebration, the hard work paid off, we did it, but for me it was bittersweet.

I have never even been to a gay wedding. I have had really good friends get married, but I think the universe is doing something, every time I get invited I have another commitment. My niece got married during COVID, but I couldn't go to the wedding, she was going to have all these people, I thought she was nuts! I don't know why I haven't been to a gay wedding yet, spiritually I think something is going on there. I am just not at that place, it's like my soul is saying "you're not ready yet, you're not ready yet," and I think it's because of my healing process over that with my partner and that part I haven't totally healed from, so if I were to go to a wedding I couldn't get into the joy, I would just get into the sadness.

I went to a friend's reception and she kept telling me to make sure I bring my hānai daughter, Keikilani, who is the granddaughter of my partner that we raised together. She kept telling me she had a special table for me, but what she didn't tell me was that my partner was going to be one of the people she recognized. She put together this PowerPoint and we watched this screen, people were clapping and it was very beautiful. Kalei was a very staunch supporter of gay marriage and the Hawaiian gay community and the gay voices in the sovereignty movement. It's a lot for me to talk about sometimes, but it is good.

Retirement

I retired in December 2017 after working thirty-two years at the University of Hawai'i at Mānoa, I was seventy-two at the time. I was ready, I had been around, and I told myself, "Been there, done that," and as an older person, you have to make room at the table so others can take over. You have to move aside and it was my time.

I had to mentor myself. Doing it alone is hard and I didn't want others to do it alone and fortunately I had the women's coffee shop. A lot of the women there would sing and dance and be happy, a lot of them were local Japanese women, professional maybe more conservative side, but playful. They expressed themselves and it was cool to hang out . . . Nā Mamo was an opportunity to organize and have discussions. We met on Sundays and people came and more people kept coming. Our living room started out with five people and soon we had twenty you know people were hungry for those discussions and talk story, eat and sometimes they never like go home you know. I remember Mono just passing out in the living room and Kalei says, "eh you goin sleep over here, ok?" "K!" and all that stuff. Back then we were able to have these discussions openly, it was really different. At first we were going to try the Gay Community Center and that was like, "no, no, you can't do that" you know, it's really different, they control the agenda over there and that's not our agenda.

Nā Mamo afforded us that experience and people went on from there. Mono is with the Harm Reduction Center and sets up policies, is a recognized leader in the community working with trans people and what's his name, Camaron Miyamoto at the UH LGBTQ Center and things like that. We went all over. Peter Silva, people in different places now, all came out of Nā Mamo and when we run into each other we celebrate it with each other you know because those were very special days and times. Sometimes people would tell me that I have a lot of power. I didn't understand what that meant, but it wasn't until years later that I reflected on it and thought, I do have a lot of power! Maybe it was good at the time that I did not know that. Sometimes they say, it's good that person didn't know how beautiful they were. Power did not phase me, I just knew I needed to share my knowledge with other people. The work to bring voice and visibility to the gay Hawaiian community was what was important.

2

Noenoe Silva
The Legacies of Nā Mamo

I am generally from the Kailua area where I lived until I was eight or so, then my mom took us to the Bay Area. I lived all around that area with different family members as I was growing up. After I graduated from high school I joined the Army and afterwards lived in Minnesota for a couple years. I got married, divorced, and then went back to California. I went to college in Minnesota but couldn't quite settle on a major, but I knew I wanted to study languages and Hawaiian. It never even occurred to me that I could apply and just come to school in Hawai'i.

I finally came home in 1985 to study the Hawaiian language. Coming home I moved into a family that I didn't know that well. I lived with my grandmother's two sisters. My grandmother had six living siblings that all lived on O'ahu. It was a huge family that I knew some people, but not everyone. My grandmother and some of her sisters were very Catholic. My mother was always fighting with my grandmother because she was basically bisexual and would have long- and short-term relationships with men and women. She and her mom never got along. She never really told me why, but my mom was really aggressive, loud, drank, and partied a lot. My grandmother was an entertainer, a dancer, singer, and she wasn't like my mom. I was reserved for a long time. I was cautious about having an opinion about anything when I first came home. It made it very difficult.

I did not really get involved in anything politically until I was teaching Hawaiian language and going to library school. I can't remember how I met Ku'umeaaloha, but she asked me to become involved in Nā Mamo. I had not been involved in any sovereignty stuff or anything up until that point. I was out on campus, I had a girlfriend. Once I decided to come out, it was easy. I was not young. At the university I saw that I knew things and was getting comfortable with who I was, at that point I was not nervous about my family, it was like whatever, deal with it.

Nā Mamo o Mānoa

I was in the original Nā Mamo when it got formed with me, Ku'umeaaloha and her partner Kalei, Nawahine and her partner, Kalaiki, and Peter Silva and James

Mould. We started adding people after that. Puakea Nogelmeier actually came up with the name. Our primary activity at first was the marriage stuff, but then we started getting more involved in the sovereignty stuff.

It was 1993. For the first six months or so, Nā Mamo was mostly doing the marriage thing. Then it started to feel like we were spending all this time talking to these haoles. We started to feel it and we were always getting into conflicts with them. There was always a conflict of style and they were so obnoxious and had this unacknowledged sense of superiority all the time. I recall a feeling of being dismissed in a meeting and feeling that some of the Hawaiian concerns are greater than this marriage thing. One time Kuʻumeaaloha got Aʻo Pōhaku Rodenhurst, sovereignty activist, to come and talk at a meeting, and the broader LGBT group that was mostly haole did not appreciate it. These people did not understand that they should be in solidarity with our other struggles. It was not just about this middle-class project of marriage. This was one of the turning points when we started thinking about talking to our own community. We thought we should start joining some of the Ka Lāhui meetings to try talk to them about what was going on.

We started going to the Ka Lāhui events, we went to the Pūwalu[1] on the Big Island. It was a whole weekend. Kēhaulani Kauanui, Kānaka Maoli professor and author, was there too. We went there and camped and strategized. We did a ton of work to show that we were really there. We did not just want to change them, we wanted to do the work. Kuʻumeaaloha gave a workshop on privilege of all kinds, we talked a lot about cis straight privilege, although we did not use that word at the time.

We worked all weekend to lay the groundwork. The weekend was structured in these different sessions to come up with a document of where to go from here in the sovereignty movement. We were doing all these things to try to prepare people for us to make an intervention at the end and say we wanted this statement added to it. For some reason I was picked to speak for the group, so I was supposed to stand and share our statement. It was resisted heavily. One of the things was that people did not want to put anything in there that was not discussed with their respective communities and talked over beforehand. One of the other things was this idea that nobody in the community is homophobic so it was unnecessary. People also did not want to show this side of ourselves to the non-Hawaiian community.

---

1. Pūwalu were a series of meetings through which Ka Lāhui Hawaiʻi was founded and operated. For more on Ka Lāhui Hawaiʻi, see *Ka Lāhui Hawaiʻi, the Sovereign Nation of Hawaiʻi: A Compilation of Materials for Educational Workshops on Ka Lāhui Hawaiʻi* (Hilo: Ka Lāhui Hawaiʻi, 1993).

They wanted us to just pretend that we're not gay. It was this whole range of objections that didn't have anything to do with each other. We were in conflict and people got really emotional and then it was like the usual we can deal with that after the revolution type of thing. Like this isn't a major issue. In our statement we were trying to say that if you allow this kind of lack of acknowledgment and recognition of the LGBT people in our community then that allows for discrimination in your new nation. You are just putting the same kinds of structures into place, which means we could be closed off from land and other kinds of things. That was in our statement.

Everyone was saying no. Then I think Skippy Ioane stood up and was like "I don't know if you guys have noticed but it's Sunday morning and we ain't at church," he went on to explain that the missionaries did this to us and that he supported what we were trying to do. And then Lilikalā Kameʻeleihiwa, it's like the lightbulb went off and she stood up too and supported us. She said that our kūpuna never had this kind of discrimination and stuff like that. This led to more discussing and listening and after an hour or something it was finally agreed to. But, at the end, it was not included. I don't know how many Pūwalus there were and even though they said they were gonna include it, it was never published. They never published anything from that Pūwalu, so there was that resistance built into the leadership. They were like, we're not even gonna make a statement about it, we are going to act as if it never happened. We were pissed.

By that fall of 1993, I was entering my PhD program and it was pretty demanding so I had to quit. It had become very stressful and maybe I was being left out of conversations because my then partner was non-Hawaiian and they were moving to make Nā Mamo only for Hawaiians. There was a meeting where we basically kicked non-Hawaiians out and after that it was difficult because she had done a lot of good work. There were some good non-Hawaiians involved, there were also some people there that you wondered about their motives, wannabe Hawaiians on there and maybe they were the problem or why that happened. But I am grateful for Nā Mamo and what I learned. It is really where my Hawaiian political activism started. That's where I met Lynette Cruz and a bunch of people that I wouldn't have met otherwise. I started doing my research two years later, starting to present at sovereignty events about my research.

Same-Sex Marriage Hearings

The same-sex marriage hearings were really hard. We were not prepared for the nastiness, we had no clue how nasty and mean people could be. You could really see some of the homophobes spending too much time in their head imagining

Island Lifestyle Magazine, January 1994. Right to left, Noenoe Silva, Peter Silva, James Mould, and Kuʻumeaaloha Gomes. Used with permission.

what gay people do. We felt like, please, we don't need these descriptions, it was horrible. The hatred that just spewed out of people was just horrible. I remember really clearly this one time at the Queen's Conference Center now on Beretania and Punchbowl, but it used to be the Mabel Smyth Auditorium. We made a hoʻokupu wrapped in tī leaf and presented it to the legislators and I was going to read our statement. I forget what, but I said something about the harms that Western civilization has done to Hawaiians and Terrence Tom, the leader of the thing, got all upset and yelled, "We'll have none of that in here!"

He didn't want to hear anything about how Western civilization had harmed Hawaiians, that this was one of the ways that this has harmed Hawaiian culture, my culture, it wasn't like this before. We were just so sick and also some of the stories that came out from couples that had been together forever that should've been allowed to be married. I remember this haole woman that was from Mānoa, she got up and talked about how she and her partner had been together for fifty years, they didn't have any protection for their home or if you know one of them died or anything like that, so those kinds of stories were really touching. We went to several hearings. In the following years I participated in others too even though I wasn't part of the group. I have this funny memory of a hearing, again at Mabel Smyth Auditorium. I parked my car and as I was walking to the auditorium, I was on the corner of Beretania and Punchbowl, at the light and the anti-marriage people were out there with their signs saying "honk if you're for traditional marriage" or something and so one of them yelled into this car going by with a man and a woman sitting there at the light minding their own business, he asks, "why aren't you for traditional marriage?" and the guy looks and he goes "because my wife used to be a man" and it was like the funniest thing to witness. It was so random, just this old lady in her muʻumuʻu.

A couple years later they did the constitutional amendment and shame on people for doing that. I think it was about that time people started to question what traditional meant and whose traditional were they talking about? I remember Kaleikoa Kāʻeo gave a really good presentation on the question: how do you say marriage in Hawaiian? And you don't! Hoʻāo just basically means 'til sunlight. There weren't that many people in the Hawaiian community talking about that. I think Leilani Basham wrote a paper on it, but it didn't get discussed that much amongst the ʻōlelo Hawaiʻi faculty aside from Kaleikoa and me.[2] It felt like people didn't want to engage with it at the time. Some people like Kēhaulani Kauanui were talking about it though. People knew that

---

2. Leilani Basham, "Awaiaulu Ke Aloha: Hawaiian Sexuality, Gender and Marriage," unpublished manuscript, 2004. Cited in Kauanui, *Paradoxes of Sovereignty* (2018).

Hawaiians did not have marriage traditionally, but it wasn't a thing that people made a big deal about, but that film, *Ke Kūlana he Māhū* was made in the '90s and a lot of it came from Kuʻumeaaloha. She was the thinker behind that and more needs to be done. It's taken from then to now to really talk about this and we're only at the very beginnings of it. More people are starting to question not just heteronormativity but monogamy because there was no such thing as one partner until you die. Some people chose that and it's fine, but it's a choice every day and you always had the choice to leave, there was never an economic reason why a woman would have to stay or even a man would have to stay in a marriage because they couldn't do whatever it was in the European and American economies that made it that you had to have a man or woman to survive. We just never had that here. From that point of maybe in the mid- to late '90s, they're starting to say, "hey, that's not how we were, we were colonized you know" but then, how do we get to saying that we want to be married? I understand it, I supported it, I support people's right to do whatever the hell they want to do. If they want the state involved in their relationship, go for it, because you get protection that way, but I think the process of getting liberated from the whole thing is a long process.

A Hulihia

A lot has happened in the wider society. With my students now, I just feel so glad for them, they don't have to put up with the kind of bullshit that we had to put up with growing up and even into adulthood. There's still rampant homophobia, it's there, it rears its head, but it's just they're so much freer in everyday activities at least the college kids I know. There's no shame factor anymore. This is allowing the next step of liberation to emerge.

Recently, on July 4th, I went to this gathering of some of our graduate students to commemorate Haunani-Kay Trask and I was trying to talk to them about the word māhū because it's been in this moʻolelo that I have been reading. This moʻolelo Kamaakamahiʻai,[3] in both versions there's adversaries, two māhū and they are Kamaakamahiʻai's adversaries. They're kupua (demigod, shapeshifter), but there's no suggestion that this has anything to do with their sexuality or their physicality in any way. They're just māhū and they have these powers. I was telling the students that we need some research about what our kūpuna imagined māhū to actually be. We talked about the film

---

3. *Ka Nupepa Kuokoa*, vol. IX, no. 40, October 1, 1870, "Ka Moʻolelo o Kamaakamahiʻai."

Kapaemāhū,[4] which is a beautiful film, I love it, it's taken a lot of poetic license and I support the reasons for doing that. I also have questions. I think māhū has evolved over time, but I don't know how we're going to find out because if you try to look for instances for the word māhū in moʻolelo it's really rare. Super super rare.

What is māhū? Way back in time, I have a speech from Antone Rosa from the Hale Nauā,[5] I forget the topic of the speech, but in part of the speech he talks about the Kumulipo and the part where humans are born for the very first time.[6] I can't remember which wā it was, but is where there's Kiʻi and Kāne and Laʻilaʻi and that's where it says "Kiʻi is māhū" of course there's so much we don't know. Antone Rosa was an educated Hawaiian at that time in the 1880s and there's a footnote saying something like although Kiʻi was māhū and a hermaphrodite, he was able to have children with Laʻilaʻi. Back then they were translating māhū as hermaphrodite, which today we could call intersex.

The ʻōlelo community can be very religious, in the '80s and '90s and still in many classes, you're gonna learn the pule and there's always a pule before eating at a pāʻina. It's pretty Christian pule, it's kind of woven into the culture of ʻōlelo Hawaiʻi for some people. I think it's been decolonized by some people and not by others. For some people church is a requirement to become part of the community, so I suspect it's all bound up with having so many people from the Niʻihau community and other really Christian communities.

When I think back to the 1990s, it really struck me at the time that there's this feeling that I had outside of the University, amongst our community, our families and communities, there is a lot of tacit acknowledgment that there's a lot of gay people around all the time, but it's not talked about. I don't know what it is, but it's not good. I think that feeling has kind of disappeared. Like one of my cousins I remember was closeted living with a woman and then, she finally gave it up and just realized nobody cared and in fact, your partner will be embraced. That's one major difference I observed from the late '80s, early '90s to now. Not only is it freer for college-age people, but something changed somewhere in our community. There's still definitely so many religious people in the Hawaiian community and so much homophobia because of it, but it's just not as pronounced.

4. *Kapaemāhū*, Kanaka Pakipika & Pacific Islanders in Communications, 2020, http://www.kapaemahufilm.com/.
5. Antone Rosa was a politican, lawyer, and judge of the Hawaiian Kingdom and the Republic of Hawaiʻi. The Hale Nauā was a society revived during King David Kalākaua's reign that promoted knowledge in the fields of art, science, and literature.
6. Hawaiian creation chant, originally composed as a name chant for Kalaninuiʻīamamao.

Why It Mattered

We did important things with the sovereignty movement, we brought up the issue. Even though it never happened, they never published the minutes from that particular Pūwalu, people from that event never forgot that and so years later, there was a panel discussion at Hawaiian studies called "Ka Leʻa o Ke Ola" and it was Kaleikoa, me, Kuʻumeaaloha, maybe Leilani. We had our panel discussion and Keliʻi Gora stood up in the audience afterwards and said, "I just want to say that we were wrong back in '96" or whenever it happened, "and that Ka Lāhui has now fully embraced LGBTQ rights" or something to that effect. They wanted us to know they have adopted a platform with LGBTQ rights even though when we brought that to them, they kept thinking about it and eventually changed it. Of course it wasn't just us, society was changing around them as well.

That was the best thing that came out of that and going on record at the legislature, being there in front of the greater community to say, "We are Hawaiian and we know we want marriage equality and we want homophobia and discrimination to stop" and to counter this kind of idea that local people aren't gay, that this was an alien idea that haole people have brought from America over here.

I hope that the liberation continues and that we continue to see and emulate the freedom that our kūpuna had around sexuality and relationships, that we can free ourselves from the constraints of what's really unrealistic to me, this unrealistic expectation of lifelong monogamy. I mean, people find ways to adapt, and monogamy is fine as long as you wake up every day and choose your partner and they choose you. But once somebody is like, I don't choose this anymore, there shouldn't be like dire consequences and murders or whatever. I just hope we keep going in that direction and that we look at how our kūpuna thought about relationships in more depth and really appreciate where their sense of freedom of their responsibilities to each other. Like, I don't want to be here anymore, okay, that's fine, you go. It doesn't have to be a big trauma, your whole economic life doesn't have to be embedded in your relationship.

Of course, we didn't really make marriage equality happen, I think that took a lot of change in popular culture. There was just so much more gayness on tv and movies, these depictions of acceptance and normalcy that pushed everything. As this became more normalized, the legislators didn't see the problem so much anymore. So, we didn't have anything to do with the eventual passing of it. For us to stand up in front of everybody and say "That's not true. We are Hawaiian and this is what we think." Those two things are probably the legacy of Nā Mamo.

3

Nawahine Dudoit
Coming Home

When I was a little girl, I realized when I was at the lighthouse, something is different about me, and I knew when I was just a little girl. When you're little, you don't know grown-up stuff. You don't have an idea, but you feel something inside that's not the same like everybody else and you don't dare say anything about it. So you have to accept yourself at first when you're really young and you know who you are and you grow up and by the time you're a teenager and you tell your mother and she wants to dropkick you over the goal line and I'm thinking, "Oh my god, Mom, no!" You can kick me as hard as you want to, but I'm still going to be fine. I know my mother loved me, it's just that she had a hard time accepting who I was. You know what, we're all different human beings just like every person who's heterosexual. I think that's what they forget and it's not about the sexual part that's important, it's just part of who we are.

I came home in 1993. I grew up in California, San Diego area mostly. The first or second week I was home, my cousin told me to come to the capital. I saw my relatives there and I heard this person yelling, "I am not American! I am not an American"[1] and I thought, "woooww who is saying that, and a female voice?" It stimulated me and I was glad to be home.

When I showed up at that first protest, I saw my Aunty Aggie sitting with some people from Aotearoa, I knew that was them because of the kākau, the tattoos on their mouth. I did not know the significance of it, but I knew they were the people of Aotearoa and I was very happy to be home after being gone for so many years. I was born in 1950, left Hawai'i in 1958. I came back and forth, my grandmother would call my mother on the telephone, "send the big girl" and that was me. I am the eldest, so my grandmother would want me to come back and one of the things she taught me is, "You must aloha everybody and treat everybody the same." I've been so fortunate in my life, everything is intertwined.

---

1. "We Are Not American" speech, Haunani-Kay Trask—Speech from the Centennial of the Overthrow, 'Iolani Palace, January 17, 1993.

My grandpa was the caretaker of the Kalaeloa Lighthouse, which is out past ʻEwa where Barber's Point was. When I was a little girl we lived there. My grandma was the glue that kept the family together, all the siblings and cousins are very close. Whenever they had pilikia everyone would get together. In fact, I just went to a funeral of one of my last uncles. We still have one aunty left of the Naʻauaos that is alive in that generation. It was so great to see my cousin. It's hard to keep in touch and have reunions like we used to, but we have to. It doesn't matter if we're māhū, it's not about that, but at least I know we respect each other. That's something I treasure and that's because of my Tūtū keeping the family close together no matter what. We are all able to forgive each other and still love one another and continue on.

Growing Up

My mother really valued education and was strict sometimes. We had to keep our mouth shut. I was a child of my mother and that's how I was raised. As a child, you do what your parent tells you. My siblings used to tell me when I became a teenager like fifteen, sixteen, seventeen, I started to buck my mother at home. They would hear my mother and I disagreeing and then they would hear a smack and so when I would come into the room where they were, they would tell me, "Don't say nothing to her, you know if you say anything that's different from her she's going to hurt you," and I tell them, "I can't help it!" All that time we grew up together, my mom told me if anything happened to my siblings, I'm going to get the lickings. I know she meant it. Even though we in California, I had to mālama them. I fought their fights. Thank God for my uncle, he taught me how to box.

On Saturdays we couldn't go out until we did a major clean-up of something, and sometimes it would be we go in our pantry and we take everything out, wash all the pantry out, all the shelves we wash it and wipe it down, and then wash everything, wash and wipe everything and put it back. Everything goes in the pantry whether it was food, cans, whether it was dishes, silverware you know and we just kept on doing the whole house. My mom wanted us to keep busy when Saturdays came, we were not allowed to watch cartoons. We had to get up at a certain time, had to help hurry up, pau eat, and then clean for about three, four hours. While we were cleaning she would put the Hawaiian records on and we would listen to Hawaiian music while we're cleaning. Sometimes I'd sing along and so we had a lot of Hawaiian music around us, a lot. ʻCause there were Hawaiian bands too up there and my brother started playing music and we started singing. When I was a girl at the lighthouse, Grandma would start washing dishes and she would start singing a song and she was the soprano, and then my auntie would come and start wiping dishes and she was the alto, and then my mom would come and she was the second soprano so they would be three-part harmony when I was a little girl. The three of them are doing different things and they're singing the same song, but every time the song is different. So I was raised, God gave me a lot of gifts, and hearing my mother and my aunty and my grandma sing was one of them.

Fighting Racism

Growing up in California, one time I had a fight with this boy because white kids were pushing us together, me and a Black boy to fight. We didn't have anything against each other and we were really fighting. I never really fought anybody like him because he doesn't give up so I resorted to being a girl and I bit him in the ear. I guess I bit him too hard, the next I saw him in the principal's office, he had this big thing on his ear and his mother was sitting next to him. My mother next to me and the principal was talking to us. We both knew we was gonna get lickens after. The lady goes, "my son has something to tell you, tell her," and he says, "I'm sorry for fighting with you," and I felt so bad and I told him, "I'm sorry for biting your ear, I never did that before," and we were trying to explain to the principal that the white boys pushed us together. Our mothers weren't listening to us. So we told the principal and we didn't get into trouble. Anyway, two weeks later I was at the movies with my friends and I went to the concessions and I saw this big gang of Black boys coming in, the first one was the one I bit in the ear. The whole gang was behind him and they were looking at me like making gestures and he shook my hand and he says hi. His gang was like oh my goodness what did he say? He apologized for fighting and I told him I understood because it was not our fault, they made us do it. I said, "you see how low they are, they make a boy and a girl fight," he goes, "but you don't fight like a girl," and that was because my uncle taught me. And he goes, "boy I never fight a girl like you before," and I knew I was gonna stop fight, I was not gonna do it anymore. I am glad I stopped. When you young, in the '50s, I think it was more racism than sexism. The bullying that happened was horrible. You just had to walk away from it.

When I was in elementary school, the teachers made me a "safety," a person that like helps kids stop running in the hallways or reports bad behavior. You were like a little guardian, you don't let fights happen and you help people you didn't even know. You bandage them up and help them get to the nurse's office or sometimes don't tell their moms if they asked. I think the other kids found out and knew they could talk to us. I was also very very good at sports because in Hawai'i you can't help it, especially when you live on the beach and you swim all the time as a kid. I was always chosen for second or third on every time, boys or girls or just you know. I never took it as a single person, it's the team, and that's how we were raised. When it's time to eat, we all eat, when it's time to clean we all clean. It's one of those kinds of things, it didn't seem hard when you were helping one another, what's hard is stopping each other from attacking each other. I don't know why that always happened. They attack us verbally or physically. I'm not kidding it's weird, more than once.

I first learned how to play tennis before I learned how to play badminton. Badminton you have to be real careful because you could really hurt yourself, going after the birdie you know. But I used to play badminton with the teachers, the gym teachers, the men, and women. I couldn't get enough competition from any of the students. In fact, there was this one group of people when we were going to high school, they were very racist and this one girl, her last name ended in like with a Du, just like mine Du, so we kinda stand close together, but I didn't like her. And her and her brother almost looked like exact twins, but her brother liked me, and I didn't know why she didn't like me, but it didn't matter because they were all racist, and they said stuff, and maybe that's why I was closer to the pōpolo kids. What happened was, when we would play games, sometimes I would hit her on purpose with the ball. The Black girls, boy they would be laughing and I would whack her because I was very good at that, people didn't realize it takes a lot of practice.

When I would play I would hit those racist girls with the ball and I'm not kidding you, you know in volleyball when you whack the ball down, and it's fast, but I was aiming for them and they would jump and I would catch them in the leg or catch them in the head and they would look at me and they couldn't do nothing. So anyway, they was scared of me after that. But it's not that I wanted them to be afraid of me, it's that I wanted them to remember we're here too, the very ones you act upon, we're here. And I think maybe that's why I did those things that coincide with standing up for being a lesbian?

Coming Out

I was out in California, me and my brother who was also māhū, we would go out together to dance. We went together but never went home together. This was before AIDS, which was so terrible. It was special to have a brother that was same as me. He had a haole lover eventually they shared a house. Funny, first time I went out with a guy, I got pregnant. My grandma always told me I would understand when I have my own. Thank goodness I had one because I was testing what the other side was like and I'm pretty sure God blessed me the very first time. That was wonderful actually, I came to understand as time went by because I was confused as a young person, you know I was confused. My mother, she gave me the time and she loved me enough even though she couldn't bring herself to say it. She told me, "I'm going to hānai this baby but we all going to raise it together," all means me, my siblings, her you know, and we did.

Now he's fifty and he's a wonderful dad and he's still close to his children, him and his wife divorced, but they're very friendly and I'm so glad that I ended up being the person I am because I gave my family different ways to view life. Just like, the first time my ex and I decided to break up, one of the first things that came out of her mouth was "well what about the kids?" and when we came together there was only two children and by the time we broke up there was a bunch, a bunch and I said, "okay I'll have a meeting with them" and it was crying "oh Auntie" because they don't know anyone but me and her and I said "you still love her forever and ever, she'll be your auntie" so every time they go camping or they have a party they call her and her partner, yea they're still part of the family, she's still Auntie. There's no such thing, it gives people a view that you can still be kind to your ex you know, you know it's ridiculous for us not to be, but then it depends on the people.

At the same time, I had a big puka, my education and the things I had missed when I was gone from home needed to be filled. I told my mother on the phone that I needed to do things and go places here in Hawai'i. Maybe even on different islands, where I'd have to fill myself with the things I missed. She was afraid for me in certain instances and she would tell me not to go certain places or see people. I was so surprised by this because she graduated from Kamehameha almost first in her class and she did not want me to get educated on what's happening with our people. But I went anyway and I am so glad that I did. I went places where I thought would be very difficult because especially in places where only Kanaka people could go, and that if you wanted to come in you would have to almost do an oli back to the one name relative 'ohana you know and I could do that but my oli was kinda not so that great but I didn't have to worry because anytime I walked up to the door, who would be there but a cousin of mine who knew me immediately, and so I never had to worry about that. As soon as they let me in they said something to somebody else and so I always had a seat and I learned quite a bit.

I also went to the University just for a very short while, but there the connections I made I also got into other parts of education that I didn't realize I needed to fulfill in order to have a larger pool of information about things that I had missed, and I was very happy. While I was doing my thing my nephew who had told me he wanted to come home and stay, he was getting his degree too, but he's my son's generation. He came here to live. He ended up being like my son, and my son in San Diego ended up being my sister's son because of the distance. Just right down the road, for real right down the road. From kinda where I live to, what street does he live on? Hala Drive. Very simple, very close and that's what I like about Hawai'i, everybody when you say things, they know where you live, where you are.

Nā Mamo

When I came home, I decided to become part of a group of people that I met because I trusted them, I knew some of them and they were gay people, the LGBTQ community, and we got with one of the biggest groups. It wasn't too long before some of us Kanaka people got together to say we have to do our Kanaka politics as well as gay rights. We had to remove ourselves from this group and we called ourselves Nā Mamo. We grew together with different age groups, different experiences, and I was very happy to be a part of it. I did nothing when I was in the continent and now I'm home and I can do things that I was curious about. One of the things I remember was being on a panel in the 1990s, and the teachers allowed us as LGBTQ because we were Kānaka to go to their school, to sit and I think it was health class, senior class, and it was one of the first times that I believe that they were allowing people to come in to talk to students. While I was there because I considered myself the kupuna, I'm the only one that wore kinda like a small mu'umu'u. I thought what the heck am I doing? I never wear dress, but that's okay so all the others were like you know everybody else was in college and here I am with this mu'umu'u on, but I thought, I don't know, what I was thinking?

So when we went there the thing that I noticed was there and I felt aloha for there, there were more than a few kids that I noticed were trying to transition into who they were, and they couldn't say anything to us, and I could see them because I'm older you know, and they were asking questions but they had to be careful because in every class there was always some guy who was ready to make fun, who was ready to say something derogatory and when they got started the teacher would remind them that we are guests in the room, and so I thought, I'm so glad because even in our family we stuck with respecting each other even somebody mad, we have to be respectful of one another eventually, even if you have to say sorry after everything, you gotta make pau but I saw so many young people and my heart went out to them because it's difficult. And especially when the boys in the back is calling "māhū, māhū" and then I stood up and I said, "My dear, I could be your grandmother and yes I am māhū," and they looked at me and I thought you know if I don't stand up, it's like we're not there.

A lot of the boys who made fun were on the football team and now a lot of football team people who are in professional football are coming out. So who knew one of those boys were saying things like that because he didn't want anyone to know his feelings, and there it's difficult when you're young, that's why there's so much suicide, people don't feel that they're loved and they're wanted by their own families and it's difficult when there's no one telling you positive things it was difficult, and so I had to be brave and stand up and say something to this boy and I glad that the teachers is kind of backing us up small kine but after that, that was enough. I thought I had to wear my nice clothes. I think the only reason I wore a muʻumuʻu was because it was Kamehameha School. When you go to certain venues, the way how you dress and the way you speak makes a big difference, so you know until they really hear what you have to say if you come in talking pidgin and then all of a sudden you switch to good English you know, then they figured "oh she had one over on me" instead of saying "she had something precious to say that now makes a difference to me." This is what I thought about Haunani, this is part of the reason I really liked her. Because Haunani spoke her honest truth and she wasn't afraid, she didn't need real boxing gloves, she had her own and yeah that's why I admired her. I didn't know we were the same age.

But that's why, when I came home I thought well this is the timing, God has always given me good timing. Then when you're there you just see things that need to be done so you go do them, that's just how it is, that's how I met a lot of people and even though for example when we were at the capitol building we were across the street and all these kids were being bussed in, it was a big protest, and it was against LGBT rights and there were a lot of people on our side that were just from Nā Mamo and we were the smallest group, there were so many other groups that were there and were so so happy to be a part of it. Kalei and I, she was another member of the group and she became my best friend. We were always at protests or at the legislature doing our thing.

Later on, we needed to break off from the bigger group because we were all Kānaka, and the group we left behind were non-Kanaka and some of them was actually crying when we had to go, they wanted to come with us but we said: "you must understand, we have work to do at the legislature with just Kānaka," and I think they understood. That's how we broke off. We needed to stand up and do our own testimony at the legislature as Kānaka and as gay people also.

Kalei and I did a lot of stuff. One time we went to San Diego and her and her partner, Kuʻumeaaloha and I went so I had them meet my family and my ex was still in San Diego so we stayed over there. Everyone asked, "what, you're going to stay with her?" I said, "it's my house k." They go, "oh it's your house, but you let her?" I said, "it's my house no worry eh but come on now." You know all of us, we

Nawahine Dudoit (left) with Kalei Puha. Courtesy of Kuʻumeaaloha Gomes.

are not like everybody else, e kala mai, we have so much shit happened to us in our life, we don't do that to other people. It would be easy to resort to being a common idiot. We have to practice in the opposite and that's what it is, all it is, is just continue to practice in the opposite. You can still tell people how you really feel. At first kinda hard to tell people how you really felt about loving them you know, because everybody misses hearing it when you're young somethings missing. Especially when you're a lesbian and your mother is not happy about who you've become. She left that part out for me and so what I did is, well, what a lot of kids do, their very best to show their parents that they're not what they think they are. But I always did that and there wasn't any change, but I tried to do more and I did. I am very glad about the things that have happened in my life but I have been very fortunate that I've been given many many gifts.

We needed a group of people who were cohesive and we had developed relationships with one another, because there was nobody else out there but us and in our culture you don't wanna make shame, but we realized there's no such thing as make shame when we cannot speak for our own. The LGBTQ aspect was not being spoken to and it was time and when we spoke up a lot of people were upset because we kept quiet for so long. We stayed down and now we're all coming up. Our cohesive group where there was always we could speak to one another if something was going on with each of us, no matter what we were saying in public. When we spoke to the public we always used things that were happening with us and why it needs to change. When it came to eventually speak of marriage, that was one of the worst topics I tell you because of course everybody would go right back to the Bible.

We didn't want to make those kinds of comparisons "well we're gonna find something in the Bible" to react to what they had said. We couldn't really do that and part of it is a lot of people in Hawai'i who are LGBTQ they still Christian too, and we all kinda have all of that even some of us still we have respect for even though we don't pray to the gods, we have respect for what our kūpuna respected. It wasn't easy to go about talking about things, carrying signs about things, because we were exposed and there was nobody out there to protect you. But, we didn't have as much fear as what's happening now and people are pushing older people down and harming them. Things that are going on now is different from what happened back then, people did not do that.

At the Hearings with Kalei

Kalei and I, we were speaking for the rights of LGBTQ people all the time that we had a chance to. Once you start talking you have to speak with conviction cause basically, we were the only two out there all the time because everybody had to go work. Kalei and I didn't have to work, so we were the two guys that our work was lege, that was our work. And we met a lot of people and we didn't always get along with everybody but that's okay. That's the reason why Kalei became my dear friend, I think we both kinda was like lean on each other. We just knew about it already, it's like you know we're cool, we're good. You look at Hawaiian girls and big kine girls, you look at them like oh butchy kine girls but you know what it wasn't, sometimes people get intimidated with the way you look, but I would think to myself, we can understand each other and still make a difference with what we're saying?

We treated people with respect and as soon as they started treating us with disrespect, they would get it. We have something to say, you have something to say, let's say it. The idea of people putting all of us, even us with all our internalized stuff going on "oh yea, you butch, you this, you that" cut it out! We all had to live and learn. And what happens is, the real thing comes out, the real thing is: we care about each other and even though we scared out here by ourselves we're gonna come back tomorrow because we're not that scared. After a while you kinda get maʻa to it, you know we weren't afraid and they knew who we were.

After a while all these guys who looked like they was tough, we all have our facade but what we really want to do it is get our message across. Sometimes you know the muscles or the whateva the costuming, that's really what it is, the costuming that people have in order to say what they have to say sometimes takes precedence on what people are going to say. Some people may pay more attention to it or not, but that facade is not the true reality of what comes out of your mouth. What came out of our mouth is that we tried to respect everybody because once we got into an argument everything was pau, everything blew up.

Kalei was Kuʻumeaaloha's partner and she was so sweet. But don't push her, don't even get her mad. She was my buddy, she was until the very end, she was the best. If I had not had Kalei there it would have been a tough road for me. I don't know if I would have been as out and open as I was, I probably would have been eventually but I got there sooner because I had somebody in my corner who was always there for me, we were buddies and we could talk about anything. She was my sister too. Sometimes I talk to Kuʻumeaaloha, I don't even realize it I'm talking about her about Kalei and I'm crying, I don't even realize it. And it's just that we went through so much different things together, we were on a lot of things in public and a lot of times was me and her because everyone else was working and so they depended on us to give them you know the stuff that was going on out there. When I was in California I never had any friends who were, over here they use more of the words butch and femme, over here they use more butchy, like that. But when I was in California they don't use those words as much, and the women that I had seen mostly were kinda like feminine looking, so when I came home I found more non-feminine women here. I became friends with them and because I didn't have them in California, I'm so glad that I have them here.

Protests

There were some people there that were from the continent, these two haole guys with their bullhorns was yelling stuff. They was almost on the verge of saying profanity across the street, and all the people across the street were kids being bussed in from high school and there were some Hawaiian entertainers that were there. They were holding their banners and we were holding ours, and it was just a protest but Kalei and I had to go to these two haole guys and say, "Brother, you know what, you're not in the continent, do you know where you are? This is not vacation time or you think you can talk to people the way you are doing that right now, you're talking to our family across the street." They were starting to get tough with us and wise with us and Kalei just got 'em, and I backed her up and I said, "you know what, you have to be respectful of people you don't know. You are no longer in wherever you came from, we are family-oriented and we take care of one another, that's our family over there, knock off the language. You can say whatever you want but leave the profanity out of it, you know watch how you talk to them," and they were, "oh okay."

And then when we walked back these kids give 'em across the street and they were getting all tough with us and they had their banners and were making any-kine and I said "eh watch what you're saying dear," and Kalei said, "we have grandchildren, what the heck are you guys talking about?" and they go "whaaaat, oh you guys māhū yeah?" and we go "yes we are, so what? You get māhū in your family?" "oh, yeah," "think about it dear, watch what you say, watch what you do," and I say, "and when you cross the street, watch for the traffic" because the traffic was bad that day, so I thought it just came out because you know, we can't help it when the kids cross the street and I thought "oh my God this is so ironic" and they go "okay Auntie" now we Auntie now! So they cross the street. So we had this incident that happened, and it happened in a few hours, less than a few hours, and we had contact with both sides and then I think we may have touched something in them, I don't know. But it's like we couldn't keep our mouth quiet because too many people stay quiet, and when Kalei and I were together something happened. Sometimes it would just be me and Kalei on one side and there would be Kānaka on the other side because they did not want us to have gay rights. Some of the people that we left from our group before we became Nā Mamo would end up coming to stand with us.

Sometimes we were there with the Hawaiians, sometimes we were together when we were doing the gay rights issues which separated us from Kānaka. It was just me and Kalei and everyone knew us. We were there every day and then one of the Aunties with us in the same big office, said something about a ride home. When they said where they were going, we knew where was that, it was on the way, and we said, "eh Auntie, you need a ride home?" she was older than us, "we can give you a ride home!" "what bebeh? You sure?" and I said, "it's no problem Auntie, come on, we go." When I came from California I had this big humongous gift and one of the gifts was a brand-new Mercedes sedan. It was beautiful and so when she sat down in my car she was like in shock, like maybe someone was taking movies of her. I said, "Auntie, everything okay?" And she was sitting in the car and she said, "you sure?" and I said, "Auntie do you want to stop and get something to eat? We can get drive thru," and she goes, "oh no, that's okay." So every once in awhile we would see her and say, "Auntie, how you doing?" and you know, "You need a ride home just let me know," and after that we became friends with everybody because we took Auntie home.

Me and Kalei was easy with everybody, we just fell into what we meant to. We family together and that's the difference about Kānaka in Hawai'i, we think about each other. We take care of one another and it's okay if somebody have something against us. We still gotta go to that meeting, we still gotta see our auntie, we still gotta go to the party even if people may not like us, so what? Cuz you know the more you show up, the more they change their mind. That's the thing. I told my nephew one time when he was very young, when we first was here, he lived with my brother-in-law and the other side of the family would treat him not good and one time he asked me how come they treated him like that. I told him to think about it and don't forget because in the future everything is going to change. I was so very proud of him, he stood up on his feet every time on his own and he came to stay with me. Things have been quite interesting, we both made our own trips. I told him, one day things will change, don't worry. From the way they treat you now, down the road they will treat you differently, don't care about them, the hardest thing is not giving up because sometimes some people are not worth your energy.

That's why by the time I started doing work with Nā Mamo, I've had enough fights in my life, I knew how to duck and weave you know, and when you're out there all alone, this is like when you're a little kid all alone and somebody tries to whack you, you have to stand up for yourself. And as an adult, you are ducking and weaving, and it's all words and attitude, a facade that you give to others as you speak, the dress that you wear, the suit that you wear, the words that you say. Then you come against the little auntie who might say just a few things and everybody looking at Auntie and then looking at you and you just lost your stand that you were standing on braddah cuz. Auntie said just a few words and she knocked you off the stand without even touching you because what she said was simple and she said it without being negative and hateful.

One of the biggest things that Kalei and I wanted to be there for was gay marriage and we spoke so much about the freedom of being married to your loved one. I guess that's the thing that people wanted to windle us down, break us down to just a sexual thing, it's like e kala mai after you get married, you never get sexual? Only us sexual, not you? We have to tell them things like that because it was obvious to us that they had managed to put us in a corner of filth, like "we don't do that!" We had to say different things that we were not necessarily comfortable with, but nobody was saying them. And I tell you sometimes I would have to go home and have a drink, actually I never drink. I would go home and have a smoke, yeah because uh gosh I was a lot calmer after a smoke.

There were a lot of Hawaiians that were pretending that they never had māhū. Number one, you know they wanted us to just shut up and listen to them, and when we listen to them they put us in a hole of filth that's what they did. No matter what came out of their mouth, they want us to be in a hole of filth because they are now going to Christianity. I used to say to myself, "God forgive them" they really don't know what the hell they're talking about. We continuously have to fight the very people we love, because that's who they represent. And you know sometimes I would say things like that and they would look at me like "you just saying that" and I was saying something that was profound, "jackass." No for real, they missed it, but if they missed it because they don't agree, they don't agree with anything that I say. They're going to miss it because they're not hearing me.

That's really what the main pilikia that me and Kalei came across, people never like hear what we were saying no matter what came out of our mouth. And we weren't too argumentative most of the time because we knew that was pono, you know, it's not gonna work if you are argumentative, but a lot of times they just never like listen. After a while you kinda grow this scab that actually becomes like armor, you have to. It would have been nice if we had more people and oh once in a while some of our gang would come up when they could and it helped. It didn't matter if it was just me and Kalei, and not because we had to, it's because we wanted to. After a while, we wanted to cause we were always there together and you know we didn't have a lot of friends, to be honest, and so it was typically us out there together. And then when we got together with the rest they would go "okay now we gonna do something else, oh we gonna go Pūwalu" "yaaay" gon get off this island for a little while.

Pūwalu

The Pūwalu gatherings were very interesting. After we had meetings with people and it was very difficult. There was a larger crew and after we would meet to decompress from all the things that were said, some days it was really hard. It was difficult because you look at the people you're speaking to and they represent your family, they represent the community, they represent everything that we hold dear here in Hawai'i. That's how I looked at it and continue to look at it, in order for me to continue to do the work. If I did not see them as my family, if I did not continue to tell myself not to be afraid, I would've given up. It's easier to give up if you don't have something to stand on and that's why I helped Kalei out because besides having myself, I had Kalei, somebody who was physically there. I did a lot of stuff on my own when I was young, so it meant a lot to have somebody else out there when I'm facing all these people and they're in suits, some of them in malos. For real, honest.

Sometimes I felt like I was in a movie, but it was real, and they're over there ready to chop me in half if I say something I don't agree with them or who I am or represent. The thing is, I had to not be afraid to face those people who were against what I stood for. They only saw one piece, they didn't see the whole. That's what people miss about local people, we're the whole flower, we are not just one or two petals, we're the whole flower and we have many petals. We make up the scent that people pay to come over here for. People don't realize. People used to talk so much about what's below the piko. What me and you do is none of their business to begin with! Everybody is making it their business! Because there weren't enough people saying things in the '90s. There were people out there walking with their picket signs who were saying bad stuff to us. Kalei and I would just stand there and look at them in the eye and say things, but not make fights. I remember this one lady would say she was afraid of my partner, even after my partner retired, jeez.

I remember one time she saw me with the sign and she asked what I was doing. I remember thinking I didn't like her attitude or the way she was talking to me. I told her to look at the sign, I am holding it for a reason, because I live it! She knew that my partner and I were together. But I only speak for myself. My partner and I are opposites, she does not like to do anything like what I been doing from the beginning when it comes to gay issues, but she knows a lot of people and likes them for what they are known for on the other side. So she and this lady both work in education, but I did not like the way that she spoke to me. I was red, I tell you. I wanted to give her a punch, but I didn't. I could never do that to anyone because I told myself I gave that up a long time ago. Now I punch with my words.

You punch with your words in not argumentative ways, because the first time you make an argument, you already lost. It's like when I bit that boy in the ear, honestly, you kind of lost already. But, in the end, I made a friend. It's funny, all these things make sense now. After things calmed down with Nā Mamo I went back to work. I first went back to work in 2000, maybe 2004 and I stayed until last year. I forget what I was doing between 2000 and 2004. I forget what year Kalei passed. After Kalei passed, things changed for me, but I think that's when things were kinda calming down as well. I don't remember the timing, to be honest I didn't realize how much that would affect me. I think that's why I stepped back and I came back to work over here, at Kalihi Kai Elementary. It is the only school that I ever worked at. When we started doing the things we were doing we never thought about marriage, we were too busy thinking about everything else because there was so many people that opposed who we were, it would piss us off. At first it was like, it doesn't matter because we're still gonna be here and we have always been here, it's historically known and so I'm thinking, pau already. I wasn't on the continent anymore, I was home. But at home, with everything going on, I had to do something. I wondered where everyone was. Maybe it was fear, everybody wanted to have a more cushy life and not worry about people not liking them. After a while, I couldn't worry about others, so I was grateful to find Nā Mamo and get involved. I went to the University for language and that's where I get in touch with the LGBTQ people.

And so, it was something like that and that's what I was maʻa to as a little girl you know and then families met together at different family gatherings. So yeah you know it's like the song "come on brah let's go grind" you know the kine, just like that. So you know when every time I came home I'm so glad that I understood everything the way I did when I left, and even when I kinda missed some stuff that's why, I know it sounds so odd and so kinda funny, but if you're from here there's only one place where they use the word "bbd's" it's right here because the brand is BVD. It's like BBD. So it's wonderful when you hear the wife thought her husband in a commercial "oh you brought the red bbd's!" and I'm thinking "I'm home, I'm not the only one who thinks like that" because people who leave and come back, it's inside of us, that we're so glad we're home, no matter good or bad, there is no place like this place really there is really no place like this place.

4

Hōkūokalani Akiu
Learning to Adapt and Survive

I joined Ka Lāhui Hawai'i to learn and understand the historic part of Hawai'i, that's when I ended up getting involved with the gay side of myself and I didn't realize that those two can go hand in hand because if you got the Hawaiian side and you understand the Hawaiian side, it was always hand in hand.

My name is Philip Abraham Hōkūokalani Akiu III, I was born in Kalihi in the year of 1950, September 1st, my birthday is coming up soon. I am the last child of the Akiu family, but I have a younger brother now, there's 13 of us. Growing up in Kalihi was not easy, we were all blue collar. Basically, the people that work in hotels and at Pearl Harbor, those kinds of hardworking people. My parents were working, basically two jobs, so much of us kids were sent off to our grandparents. And lucky thing, had all my grandparents alive, so either I was in Wai'anae, Nānākuli, or Maui.

When I got older my dad felt I was getting a little too Hawaiian. To him, Hawaiians were lazy, on welfare, having lots of kids, going nowhere. He took me out of the Leeward Coast and put me in town where I had to learn to adapt to city life. Not going to the beach all the time, studying, trying to be a good, what they called "hapa-haole" kid. I had to learn to be adapting. In school, I wasn't a very good student. I always got into fights. You name a school on O'ahu, I've been to it. Benjamin Parker, Ka'ahumanu, Ala Wai Elementary, Wai'anae, Washington Intermediate. Eventually something clicked in me and I knew I had to finish, get my education down. I had a choice of going to Kamehameha, but I did not want to wear a uniform, I hated whatever that meant by wearing a uniform at Kamehameha Schools. My parents put me in Kaimukī High. My dad let me choose.

I was in choir and then my dad decided to put me into ROTC, for the Air Force. He still felt I needed some discipline. I joined Civil Air Control. And of course, I had to go to meetings and tings li'dat. My dad didn't worry 'cause he knew exactly where I would be. He would call the school and talk to the teachers to see if I was there. Of course those things I would never miss, but other subjects, I got to

LANDMARK GAY RIGHTS DECISIONS

RULING MAGNIFIES CALL FOR SAME-SEX MARRIAGE

RITZ-CARLTON
Condo builder may buy adjacent property

A second tower could merge with first luxury building

By Andrew Gomes
agomes@staradvertiser.com

Sales were strong last week for condominium-hotel units in a planned Ritz-Carlton tower in Waikiki slated to start construction this summer, so why not build another one?

That's what the developer of the Ritz-Carlton Residences Waikiki Beach is considering.

Los Angeles-based PACREP LLC is exploring the feasibility of buying land next to its 38-story Ritz-Carlton project and developing a second condo tower that could be annexed to the first tower.

PACREP disclosed the possibility to buyers in a disclosure document for condo sales.

Jason Grosfeld, a PACREP principal, declined to elaborate on the idea. "We're considering our options," he said.

According to the disclosure document, PACREP may elect to develop an adjacent tower as a separate condo or merge it with the Ritz-Carlton tower and possibly give owners in the second tower access to amenities and services in the first tower.

The adjacent lot being eyed by PACREP is owned by Food Pantry Ltd., an affiliate of kamaaina grocery retailer Foodland Super Market Ltd.

Food Pantry's lot is a little under 1 acre, or 38,000 square feet, and was once part of the old Magoon Estate that was sold off in pieces in the 1990s and led to the development of the luxury retail complex 2100 Kalakaua, also known as Luxury Row, and the Ritz-Carlton tower.

Please see **TOWER**, *A9*

Advocates vow an effort to get a state law passed next year

By Derrick DePledge
ddepledge@staradvertiser.com

The drive for gay marriage in Hawaii will intensify after the U.S. Supreme Court ruled Wednesday that gay couples legally married under state laws are entitled to federal tax and health care benefits.

The court ruled that states must follow constitutional guarantees but otherwise have the historic and essential authority to define marriage. The decision struck down the federal Defense of Marriage Act, which had recognized marriage as between a man and a woman, as a violation of equal protection under the Fifth Amendment.

Waving rainbow banners and American flags, dozens of gay and civil rights advocates held an evening rally at the state Capitol to celebrate the court's ruling as another step toward equality and to demand that Gov. Neil Abercrombie and the Legislature approve gay marriage next session.

Hawaii allows same-sex and heterosexual couples to enter into civil unions and receive the same rights, benefits and responsibilities of marriage under state law, but

Please see **DECISION**, *A8*

THE PARTICULARS

Two landmark Supreme Court rulings Wednesday bolstered gay marriage rights. Some details:

THE DECISIONS:
In one case the court said legally married gay couples are entitled to the same federal benefits available to straight couples. It did not comment on whether gay couples should be allowed to marry, leaving that up to the states. In the other case, it cleared the way for gay marriages to resume in California, where voters banned them in 2008.

BENEFITS TO BE GAINED:
There are more than 1,000 federal laws in which marital status matters, covering everything from income and inheritance taxes to health benefits and pensions.

STATE LAWS:
Gay marriage is legal in 12 states and the District of Columbia, representing 18 percent of the population. When gay marriage resumes in California, making it the 13th state, the figure will jump to 30 percent.

Source: Associated Press

Honolulu resident Hoku Akiu held American and rainbow flags during a rally at the state Capitol on Wednesday in support of the U.S. Supreme Court's rulings on the Defense of Marriage Act. See more photos at staradvertiser.com.

INSIDE

>> **What's next?** Groups prepare for state-by-state battles over marriage. A6
>> **Analysis:** Decision follows a dramatic shift in public sentiment. A6
>> **Hawaii case:** The ruling could bolster the chance to overturn state's same-sex marriage ban. A7
>> **Our View:** Hawaii is ready for marriage equality. A10

JAMM AQUINO / JAQUINO@STARADVERTISER.COM

Hōkūokalani Akiu, June 27, 2013. Courtesy of the *Honolulu Star-Advertiser*.

know an instructor and he liked to go surfing. He would pick up guys that looked good and would say anything and we would cut out of school and go surfing when the surf was up. This was in high school. Then I graduated and joined the military, got out in '73. I have no understanding of how I made it through the military. My attitude towards the military was bad. Maybe somebody, ke Akua (God), was looking after me 'cause I should have gotten court-martialed so many times. The things I used to say to people, you just shouldn't say, but I guess they thought I was kind of cute.

All my officers in charge were women and it was interesting looking back on that and looking at what was happening to me later in Nā Mamo. It was all women-led, so hello! They really did let me have freedom, as long as I knew what I was doing. I could say all kine stuff as long as I did my job. I got out in '73, bummed around for one whole year trying to figure things out, meet up with my family. I didn't meet all my family 'cause I had the Hilo side of my mom and the Kona side of my mom, all I met with was Kauaʻi, Maui, and Molokaʻi. I didn't realize my mom and dad had a huge side family too. Once I finished bumming around, I ended up going to school and there was a conflict with my dad. He did not think I should get a college education, he thought I should be working. He was happy to be a firefighter, but I felt like there was more than just being whatever, I wanted something more. I started going to Leeward Community College and this created a conflict between my dad and I, so I had to quit college and go to work.

For me coming back from the mainland it wasn't being Hawaiian, being gay, being everything else, I needed to survive. I needed to work. Do I get a GI bill and go to school? How much of it do I save to pay for living if I move out? When you come down to it, Hawaiian stuff, being gay, was out the window. I had to figure out how to survive. How do I find a job? What kind of places will hire me? Again, it wasn't about being Hawaiian. Hawaiʻi has this thing sometimes they didn't care, they just needed bodies, so they hired everybody. Sometimes it was race-related. Are you Chinese or Japanese? So I got my first job through my sister-in-law because she was working at the camera shop. She's Japanese, so she introduces me to the boss and the majority of the workers are all women and Asian looking, very fair. Here I come and they thought I matched with what the touristy-type like. I ended up working for a private company called Island Cameras and Gifts. It was in Waikīkī, I worked in the shop for about five years and then they opened up at the Kodak Hula Show. It was pre–Nā Mamo, pre-hula, pre-sovereignty. I worked there as a shop manager, watching the hula, talking to the dancers that were mostly older women and listening to their stories. I listened to Uncle David, he was the guy who climbed the coconut tree during the Kodak Hula Show. I listened to him saying how fortunate he could have a job like that. Then again, I looked at him, it's so stereotypical of what they think about Hawaiians. When we climb coconut trees, what do they think about that?

American? Hawaiian? Māhū?

The transition of coming back was difficult. I ended up working at Maluhia Hospital as a communications operator and from there I met people and transferred to the juvenile hall which I liked because I could connect with the rough and tumble attitude. I could relate to the kids, most of them Hawaiian kids. I found out one of them was my nephew. I started working for the State, I think I was twenty-two. I worked at the OCCC (O'ahu Community Correctional Center) and that lasted about a year because I couldn't keep my mouth shut. Working for the prison is a very closed society because you work with prisoners and if you see anything wrong, you're not supposed to say anything because your life would depend on your co-workers. I saw some of the injustice about the court system and I opened my mouth. From there I ended up working for UH. A lot of times when I applied for jobs the first thing they would ask is if I was born here and that would get me in the door. I worked security, another time I worked an office job. I tried to adapt, sometimes there was too much dysfunction. It wasn't always easy to adapt because I had to, I was reminded of that song, "You gotta know when to hold 'em" by Kenny Rogers.

During that time I was also going through my sexual identity thing. So, trying to be Hawaiian, understanding what Hawaiian meant and trying to understand what's happening with me on my identity as being a gay person or as they say, māhū. It wasn't easy, everything was on like a fine line. When I stayed with my parents, even though I was old enough, I couldn't listen to rock 'n roll music. My dad would literally come into my room, pull out the plug, and tell me I had to listen to Hawaiian music. He was stuck on the Christian stereotype that men don't dance hula. Back then, people would think hula dancers were all māhū, and of course, his son couldn't be māhū, I'm straight and narrow, so talk about confusion! I was trying to be "American" but not yet accepted as being American. When I was in the Air Force I was stationed at Mississippi and when I was growing up, had all those riots. We would hear the N-Word a lot, my dad used it and I wondered how he could do that. So it wasn't only that, but being gay, being Hawaiian, understanding that these words are not appropriate, going to school learning that, and trying to get a job living in Hawai'i.

Being an American was not an easy time for me. It came down to being who I was as a Hawaiian, that was the first thing I identified with, so I had to go to school to learn my language, to be my culture. My kumu hula was Kimo Alama Keaulana. Of course there was also Noenoe Silva. One of the other teachers before was Aunty McKenzie and she was a specialist in law, so she would talk to us in English, she taught us how to interpret when we talking about land divisions. Hawaiian land divisions they didn't talk about land parcels, it was like coconut tree to this rock, so that was how you identified your property. It was hard. When I was in Kimo's class, I started to get maʻa to learning and understand Hawaiian language and all its meanings and different kinds of things. One of the classes he taught was dance and he was very patient with us.

When Hōkūleʻa came, that's when I really started getting proud of who I was and that there were other Hawaiians, there's this whole mess of different colors of us being Hawaiian. Even though our last name can be Smith or Nakamoto, the main thing that we all got back was being Hawaiian. I immersed myself in everything that I could Hawaiian. Leaving that other side of me, the gay side outside the door, until I could figure out who I was first. When I finally felt comfortable in the Hawaiian side, I joined Ka Lāhui Hawaiʻi to learn and understand the historic part of Hawaiʻi, that's when I ended up getting involved with the gay side of myself and I didn't realize that those two can go hand in hand because if you got the Hawaiian side and you understand the Hawaiian side, it was always hand in hand.

Being gay, being this second part of you, was part of being Hawaiian. Being Christian or American was not easy. I was in major conflict. I could dismiss the American side really fast, but when it came down to the religious side, I had so much conflict. I went through the whole ritual of being a good Catholic, Christian young man. Holy Communion, the whole gambit. It was really a struggle to listen to my mom and dad, saying about God and church and everything else. My parents were religious, but more on the Hawaiian side, so that's why there was a conflict within me, wondering how can they be this Christian-Hawaiian, but not accept the other side?

Joining the LGBT Community

I ended up doing everything on the sly. I joined the LGBT Community Center and was part of the board. A friend of mine introduced me to it, there was a house on the side and that's where they had little meetings. Wayne Akana was the one who introduced me. He was outgoing and he just, you know, convinced me to watch the meeting and these typical meetings, you go say hello and next thing you know you're elected! I was like what?! Looking back, I was on the board for almost like fifteen, sixteen years.

This is how I ended up meeting all these people and getting involved with the LGBT community, meeting strong women, and understand that within the gay community and LGBT community, there's certain prejudice within our own community. Some people don't like transgender, certain people like lesbians, some people don't like the gays, and I could not understand. Talk about confusion! When I was going to meetings they wanted us, board members, to be part of all these other community things. I did not want to get picked because I was worried I wouldn't be able to check my mouth, or not tell people they were all wrong. Isn't this supposed to be Hawai'i and aren't we supposed to be acting better instead of having all these differences? A good friend of mine, Ken Miller, who lives in Thailand now, he used to be director of The Center, we used to have talks and I would fight with him all the time because his direction was marriage equality and I still had conflict with that.

It was the American-Christian thing. It never affected me because I was not going to get married to another person in that way. At my first protest, it was at Smite Hall by Queen's Medical Center and the religious guys were out there. At that time I still wasn't belonging to Nā Mamo. That was the first time I protested for marriage equality and that was the first time I ever had a religious person come up to me and say that I was going to hell. It was a haole person and my head starting clicking and again, you guys are telling us brownies how to act? How to behave in the white man's way? I said no more. I knew I also had to be very firm with my dad. How do you say that to your own parents? I remember telling my mom off one time, she got hurt for a whole month she wouldn't talk to me. I said, "Well, Mom, I'm not that small little kid anymore, I'm an adult." I could talk to her about anything except being gay. Once I was into the LGBT Center, that's when I branched out. I was already doing hula, doing Hawaiian Studies, so there was no problem being Hawaiian, then I got to the point about joining Nā Mamo at UH Mānoa.

Nā Mamo

Ken Miller was executive director of The Center and he told me about this new group coming up at UH Mānoa. He had heard about Kuʻumeaaloha and all the people getting involved, he encouraged me to join and see what the group was up to. I went to the first meeting, met all of them, and den didn't even realize that Nawahine, who was there, was my hula sister! When we saw each other, it was like, how strange we never talked about it? When we are in hula, nothing was said and it was kind of confusing, like that was a different side. We attended meetings and we worked on a mission statement on how to be inclusive with the rest of the LGBT. All these people started coming, one of them was Rae Watanabe, she was another influence on me. There was a whole bunch of non-Hawaiians in the group.

When it came down to that split between, and I could see it because Ka Lāhui, Haunani's side, was talking about that too. The idea was, how can Hawaiians be Hawaiians if we have outside support? Even though it's allies, as they call it, how can you say this is a Hawaiian movement, led by Hawaiians, without any outsider incursion?

So, ultimately Nā Mamo decided that we would break off. I think it was at a meeting at Kuʻumeaaloha's house. We were talking about it, that it had to be led, owned, everything Hawaiian, so all these people had to leave. I was like, "How do you do that?" I remember one meeting we had we were trying to get a Hawaiian group to recognize us, I don't remember if it was Lilikalā or Haunani. They could recognize us being Hawaiians but they could not recognize us being a LGBT organization, even though we were historically part of everything. That was very disappointing. I am not sure if Haunani acknowledged us. I remember having a talk with her when we had our protest at Waikīkī beach. We went to protest when Clinton came to sign the Apology Bill. I asked her why the māhūs not being recognized? And she went, "What, you mean the haole māhūs?" and I said "No, the Hawaiian māhūs," and she just looked at me and walked away. And right there I was ready to leave Ka Lāhui Hawaiʻi because I said, how can I join a group when they don't acknowledge this thing? But I'm like, I was so far deep into that, 'cause I was part of—each district had a group—so I was part of the Waikīkī district group. I was an officer within the group. I'm so involved inside this thing, even though my family didn't care about it, I said I want to be part of this.

There was a lot of drama in Nā Mamo. I think it was with the women. With the guys, 'cause it was a women-led organization, we sort of stepped back and said, okay, whatever you guys do, we'll follow. So they did. This one time we went camping and the difference between the women and the men really got pronounced. The meeting started off really good, we all shared our manaʻo about what we wanted from the retreat, where we would like to see Nā Mamo go, if we would like to be a formal group within UH. But I got corrected at the meeting for saying "us guys" and it felt like the women felt the men were causing a lot of the problems. I wanted to move on from these things. One thing I learned in hula was when our kumu decided to change something, you had to learn it right there, we adapt. Basically, for me, I adapted to how it's supposed to be. Within Nā Mamo, I wanted to understand why I was getting feedback aimed at the guys and I did not know of it, was just rumors.

I was the oldest of the men in the group so I was asked for my expectations from Nā Mamo. I was there because it was Hawaiian and I am attracted to strong women that know what direction they want to take. It doesn't have to be polite. We tell the university we're an organization of Hawaiians. If this is supposed to be an open campus for Hawaiians, then do so, be that way. I wasn't very comfortable when they was talking to me sometimes. They were polite but very adamant of what they wanted. As a guy, my point of view was if was me talking, I would punch 'em out first, then talk later, but that's a whole different thing. Anyway, being with Nā Mamo, I met, I love Kuʻumeaaloha. I understood and I loved where her directions were going and I'm not sure if some of the women were comfortable about that, 'cause the last meeting that I went to was at their house and when the last meeting came there wasn't that much of us with Nā Mamo. Nā Mamo lasted about five years. I started getting involved with other things at the LGBT Center. I was going to school and started to understand and do research on where LGBT people live when they get old. My role in Nā Mamo started waning.

Hula

There were all these clubs. I actually got involved with a church group for gays and they introduced me to all these things. And also, my hula brothers. My alakaʻis on my hula side, they were very gay and they were also classical dancers, like ballet. So they did their motions in that way. I respected them being alakaʻi and so I always ended up being in the back. I remember I invited my mom to our first hōʻike. We chanted and danced and when I went back to my table my mom was crying, she was so proud that I was the first of all the children that was immersed in Hawaiian culture. My mom played Hawaiian music, she was an entertainer, she did all these things. In fact, I was going through my papers and I found a poem that she wrote for me because of it.

My hula brothers would all go to the clubs. Kawika Trask would be entertaining, one of our hula brothers would ask me to bring so and so 'cause we were going out dancing. I never liked dancing in public, but they love the limelight and the first time I said yes when they called, I literally stood up and walked outside. I did not want to dance in front of anyone. Eventually they got me to. I didn't want to hear negative things about the hālau and especially against the kumu hula. I would feel hurt at some of the gossip because I think the kumu was Scandinavian or something, and every time we would go out to dance at Hawaiian things, first thing they would look at him and be like, what is this?

But my mom would talk to him in Hawaiian and she gave him the approval. Then he got married to the assistant, which was interesting because he was very flamboyant and I learned about another aspect of the LGBT community, being bi. All my hula brothers and sisters would do stuff on the side too. I was like, do you, whatevers. They enjoyed themselves and I'm like hey, our LGBT is a wide spectrum. The main focus is that being Hawaiian, how true is he to being

Hawaiian? When he invited his kumu to see our first dance, we were all kind of nervous because the kumu who transferred all his knowledge to our kumu was coming to see us. We had to be on spot. It doesn't matter if you haole or whatever, we all dance Hawaiian. It was great. People were already talking. The Hawaiian community was like, "that's the haole one" of course. What made it really really bad was when the AIDS epidemic happened, we were losing hula brothers right and left.

Five of my hula brothers passed away. I was gay but I never got too involved with going to the clubs. The only time I would go was with my hula brothers, I never really got involved with that scene. When my hula brothers started getting, dying, and they were all dying from AIDS. I think after that fifth one that's when my kumu made a statement, it was very unfortunate, he said, "I will never let another gay person into my hālau," and I was like, I love hula, I cannot see myself with another hālau. I wondered how I could overlook this. I continued dancing because he was a good teacher and I let it go because that was his opinion and all you can do is aloha.

UH LGBT Commission

When I was working, before I retired, I was involved with the UH LGBT Commission with Camaron Miyamoto, working to be recognized up there as an organization. We had a meeting with the UH president. Again my mouth always got into trouble because, they kept on putting us off. No we can't meet with you guys because of this. And, I mean majority of the people that was on that group, was all professors. I was the non-professor. The students couldn't be there all the time, so I was the only full-time staff in that group. Whenever I had a meeting I had to say to my boss that I had a meeting at UH Mānoa. They were trying to integrate gay people into the entire university system, so they let me go to this meeting. So we had a meeting to meet with UH President Mortimer. We all got there, we're all sitting down and waiting, and a lady comes out and tells us the president can't come and see us. We tried like five times. Somebody asked me what I thought and I said, "Well, let's put it this way, if it was a Japanese group, do you think they would have postponed 4 or 5 times?" We eventually had our meeting and got recognized. I worried about what I said, but Camaron never said anything. At that point, I didn't care, I wanted them to stop pushing us around.

They sent us letters recognizing us at our individual campuses and certified us as a group, as a board of LGBT and was a recognized representation of their campus. The letter said that if we needed to go to a meeting, we could go. Like holy cow, the letters were signed by the president. It's interesting, all of them was professors, I think I was the only Hawaiian in that group, only staff. I don't understand how Kuʻumeaaloha wasn't part of it. I think the mission goals of both organizations were different. One was to recognize all, every aspect of the LGBT, in sports, teaching, whatever, students, housing. As Nā Mamo was basically Hawaiian, and I think we were talking about tuition free because there's ceded lands up at Mānoa.

That part was confusing for me with Nā Mamo and The Center, trying to figure out how come they don't get together. The Center wanted a meeting with Kuʻumeaaloha Gomes because they wanted her to be part of the organization. They told me that everyone on the board was afraid of her! She's not a dumb woman, she's very educated and understands all the aspects. She had conflict with The Center too. She asked me why I would belong to a white man's organization and I told her that we not only working with one group, but we working with every group. All the LGBT community is connected with everything—marriage, housing, you name it, work, we can get fired from that! We need to work and that's why I belonged to this thing, 'cause it was tearing me apart because whenever they wanted a Hawaiian to testify they would ask me. I understood why, hello, suddenly brown became fantastic, right?! I asked my mom to testify one time, but they kept changing the meeting time and so it was 1 o'clock in the morning. When I looked there wasn't that much people. My mom testified at 1 o'clock in the morning and called them very inept politicians. My mom got little bit upset, but I didn't realize the politicians were going to do this. So, I learned more the political side of these things. For me, having my toes in all these things gave me a different aspect of it and I was still learning to be a Hawaiian. I accepted myself as being an LGBT person, I don't get accepted being called māhū. I'm married, we've been married for seven years now. My older sisters knew about me, some other family members they don't care. I have a cousin that lives on 9th avenue, she's going to go into treatment, she's transgender, she's going through the operation. I have been helping her out, going to doctors and stuff like that. Being in organizations like Ka Lāhui, Nā Mamo, we have fantastic women out there. The women side, always thinking about community, always thinking about Hawaiʻi. How we can improve Hawaiʻi without damaging our ecology, our environment, our keikis, our history.

Ka Lāhui did not recognize same-sex marriage. I think they were dealing with their own religious aspects internally. I don't think many of them were married, but they were very vocal in the community about certain things. But that was what the Hawaiians were looking at, did Ka Lāhui support it? The Center was seen as a haole-based idea, they weren't based on Hawaiian values. Basically it was all, what can the white man get. I caught flak for being involved with The Center. I didn't care. When someone white gets into my face and thinking they can bully me because I'm brown and they think they have a little bit more education than I do, I stand my ground and I educate them in what Hawaiian is about, what Hawai'i is about. My partner, whenever I get on my pedestal, he's in the background going sideways. I didn't educate myself about Hawaiian stuff to let it go! There's so much misinformation.

I got flak from the Native groups for representing LGBT, but how do I get us noticed, that we are part of this community? We are part of Hawai'i. It wasn't easy, UH hadn't recognized us yet. And now there is this whole kupuna side, trying to talk to other kūpunas. They ask, "oh your kids must be really nice" and I'm sorry, I don't have kids! They ask how come and I tell them I am married to another man, and their eyes just go big and then you know, they walk away. One of the good things with me being part of all these organizations, I was a veteran, a Hawaiian, mixed-blood, whatever. Maybe if I was more educated I would have used nicer words, I would have been more diplomatic, but I couldn't when I saw something that was not right. With the Hawaiian groups I watched other people be undiplomatic. I would sometimes think that these people were not old enough to say these things. Older people than you understand and you have to learn to listen to what they're saying and then draw your own conclusion. You listen to both sides and that's what I did. When come down to Nā Mamo or Ka Lāhui, I saw the good side of both. I wanted to bridge with the LGBT Community Center.

I am grateful I got involved in those things. It made me better understand both sides of the Hawaiian and LGBT struggles we had to go through. The majority of us were in the closet during Nā Mamo. I remember asking about where we could have meetings. I asked my mom if they could come down to 'Ewa to have a meeting. Because it was a political group, she said no. She thought it had too much power and she believed things attached to people and she did not want that to be left at the house. I mean, you talk about being Hawaiian, there are certain cultural things that goes along with it. I am grateful for that. For me, when I invite people over, especially for parties and stuff like that, I am careful. I was talking to one of my kumus and they told me to send blessings and be open to whatever comes along.

Surviving

Being a kupuna, I thought I wouldn't make it, the men in our family, our age that we would live to be about 60. 'Cause all of us share alcoholism, smoking, overweight, you name it, my men's side of my family has it. I saw many of my family dying off early, it put a little thing in my head that I have to start doing certain things and behave yourself. And the thing about acting appropriately, if you LGBT, you know there's a conflict.

But I managed. When I first moved in, my neighbors cracked me up because one came and asked about us, if I moved in with another guy. I told them that we lived together and I wanted my neighbor to say it. "Oh so you guys own the house together?" and I went, "Yeah because we both work and we live in the same house." So that is means what? Labels. I have not been shown prejudice here. There's a gay couple down the street, I say "hi" to them and I get no acknowledgment whatsoever. But when they got married they were running around here saying they got married. I try to be friendly, but they just run in the house. But if something happens, do they want my support or not? For me and my partner, who is very closeted, I say hello to everybody. I sit on the deck, having my coffee and I say good morning to everybody. In the back of my head, I remember my dad used to do that. Oh god. I invite the neighbors and they come over and have some coffee with me.

I had to adapt, I had to be at times un-Hawaiian and go back and forth. Just like when you speak pidgin you can go from one side to the other and that's basically what I had to do. When I worked for a private firm I had to be this haole side, talk nice you know, and then throw in some Hawaiian just to be this funny guy and other stuff. When it came down to my parents, Hawaiian side, that was conflict because how much Hawaiian do you have to act? How much Hawaiian do you have to be? I am Hawaiian, but you don't act Hawaiian? And sometimes went I went down to Waiʻanae, that's when I got really told, you don't act Hawaiian, and I had to respond, "What you mean I don't act Hawaiian?" They would say that I talked different and had this haolefied attitude. I asked them, "How in the world did I get that? How do I act with you guys?" I started to understand why, because when I used to drive down there, I'd come down and my mom told me afterwards, she asked if I brought something when I go to the family house? But I just get out of the car standing there looking at them instead of saying hi. I was like standoffish. My cousins were too though, so that fed into it.

Another thing being kupuna, sometimes I see one of the neighbors that comes down to have coffee, we have to watch out for each other and try not to be so hard head all the time. That's the other thing when I was going to school for social work, I focused on gerontology on the kupuna side, I was advocating. On the veteran's side I was doing the GI and the LGBT side, all the way up, I was always advocating. My boss would ask how many organizations I belong to? Sometimes my jobs would be surprised by how many things I did. I would have to come out at the VA as gay, I had to tell the LGBT that I am Hawaiian, and so on. Being adaptable and working through the system allowed me to be involved in certain things. I was grateful, but within individual groups there were challenges. Each group had its own dynamics and personalities. I sort of adapted and learned how to speak and listen and just hope that it carries on.

That's how I survived, trying to prioritize what was most important to me. First was work, after that was being Hawaiian. I went back to school to learn the language. I would talk to my mom and she couldn't understand. As a native speaker she did not catch what I was learning on the college side. Then I remember my aunt was teaching Hawaiian, she's from Niʻihau, Mileka Kanahele. She was learning but she spoke from the Niʻihau side. Someone said she didn't speak good Hawaiian and when I told her, she went and explained about our family. That's the thing, not too many Hawaiians toot their horn, you know we're kind of reserved, we don't say too much. Then when they find out, oops they put their foot in their mouth. Talk about learning and adapting and trying to be in this Hawaiian.

These days some of my old friends on Facebook talk about coming back and I asked them why if they have a family, a job, and a home that they love? Because it's hard to live here with getting constantly into arguments about financial stuff. I am strong in what I believe in, happily married and just being up here in Pālolo Valley. Go up in the mountains and go drink my coffee on the deck. Nā Mamo was an integral part of my education, developing who I was as a Hawaiian. Ka Lāhui helped me to understand my history of who I was. Hula helped me relearn the language, the culture, the yin yang side of the hula. How to be feminine, how to be strong. Educating people if they said something wrong about Hawaiʻi, knowing full well that you have knowledge on your side. Being strong in the LGBT, without going, what you said? I think for me, I'm seventy, going to be seventy-one soon, my life has been full.

5

Kimo Alama Keaulana
If you're nails, I'm the hammer and you're going to get it!

I am Kimo Keaulana, I was born and raised in Mānoa Valley. I attended Mānoa Elementary School until the sixth grade and then I went to Kamehameha Schools and graduated in 1973. From there I went to Honolulu Community College, but I left and went into the work world. I returned to school later and loved it. After I finished, I went UH Mānoa and got a Bachelor's in Education and a professional diploma in Education and a Master's in 1992. I taught in the DOE for ten years, went into the UH system first as a lecturer at Kapiʻolani Community College and then at Honolulu Community College. In 1997 I ended up being a Hawaiian Language and Hawaiian Studies assistant professor there. I also taught at UH Mānoa for about ten years in the Hawaiian Language department and in the Music department for Hawaiian Ensemble courses. I retired from Honolulu Community College about three years ago and now I am at Punahou School as their kumu of ʻIke Hawaiʻi and kumu hula.

Growing Up

Growing up in Mānoa's in the late '50s and '60s, and even the '70s, it was largely Japanese. I lived on Halelani Drive and when I grew up, Mānoa Road was just a road. There were all these hau trees and then just lots of Japanese farmers. Up in the Valley had aqua ponds and they grew ginger and tī leaves and things like that. Then they bulldozed all the farms down and created Mānoa Gardens and it became predominantly Japanese. When I went to Mānoa Elementary School it was predominantly Japanese and a couple Hawaiians and a sprinkling of others. The teachers were terrific, multi-talented. Mānoa Elementary was the best elementary school in those days. I can see why, the teachers were excellent. I wish I got more out of school. It was interesting because I never really cared for school but then I became a teacher. When I was young, school was school, I did not really love it or look forward to it. School was like whatever.

Kamehameha was really interesting to me. First time in my life I was around people my age that were Hawaiian. Up until then my classmates were largely

Japanese, so at Kamehameha it was like, "oh, this is what Hawaiians are like," you know kids my age. It was a private school and more regimented. I liked the vibe of being amongst a lot of Hawaiian kids. When we went into ninth grade, in those days, Kamehameha was a military school, the ROTC was there and it was literally 24/7. I also had a sharpshooter's medal from when I was a senior in high school. So you know don't piss me off 'cause if I have a gun in my hand and you running away from me I can pretty much shoot you to your heart, but don't take it personally. There was a time I thought I might join the military, but there were better things in front of me that were inviting. I did consider it.

I also got to know Dr. Donald Mitchell, who was very instructional in sharing Hawaiian things like the Hawaiiana Mobile, they called it at that time. I became his assistant. He was a fascinating and smart man, he wrote the book *Resource Units in Hawaiian Culture*. That's how we can play Hawaiian games and all that today, because of him. That was actually the things I looked forward to at Kamehameha because we had these things in common. At the Royal Mausoleum, used to be Aunty Lydia Namahana Maioho, she was there for 40 years. People would go to see her and she would tell people, she knows what I look like naked. Just to shock people, but then she would tell them that she used to babysit me and change my diapers. I was surrounded by these kinds of people.

I'm not saying that I wasn't called māhū, tilly, sissy, mary alice, 'cause actually I was. When I went to Kamehameha School people did not do hula like they are doing now, especially if you one boy. I would get, matter of fact, every day someone would call me something. I think I knew that I was secure and I knew there people who loved me and I didn't give a crap. I was always that kind of person. I don't give a damn who the hell you are. If you're nails, I'm the hammer and you're going to get it!

Years after I graduated from Kamehameha School somebody who would call me names in school actually came up to me and apologized. He started to dance for Robert Cazimero, his name was Reggie Keaunui. He came up to me and asked me to forgive him and apologized for calling me names when I did hula in school. He explained that now he danced for Robert Cazimero. I forgave him. He gets it now, he's actually one of the dancers in the Consolidated Theaters video they play at the movies. If it had not been for those adults and kūpuna that were in my life and validated my life, it would have been different.

I kind of liked it, but Kamehameha was not an inspiring school. It didn't do much to want me to attain academic excellence or anything like that. But, the best thing that I got out of that was meeting Aunty Nona Beamer. She and her family were very close with my mother's family. I was very involved in chanting and hula and music, so me and Aunty Nona had that in common, so that was lovely. My

Kimo Alama Keaulana. Courtesy of Kimo Alama Keaulana.

Hawaiian language teacher was Mrs. Sarah Quick, now she's Sarah Keahi. She was absolutely wonderful. I grew up with both Hawaiian and English so that was really interesting. When the Hawaiian renaissance came I was like, what? What is all this?

I think I lived a pretty much authentic Hawaiian life amongst people who spoke Hawaiian, they did things Hawaiian, they were unashamed of being Hawaiian and that's how I grew up and was inspired by these people. When I look back I really didn't have friends my age, they were largely people that were my parents' generation or even my grandparents' generation. They were nurturing lovely people. I never grew up with any kind of shame about anything. I was blessed in that respect. They saw talent in me, the ability to 'a'apo or I can grasp things quickly and hang out with them. They taught me a whole bunch of stuff. I think as far as my growing up years went, it was just filled with all kinds of Hawaiian lore and beautiful, beautiful people. I was lucky.

Entertainment

I really made no concerted intent on becoming a singer or an entertainer. I did not wake up one day thinking, I really want to do that. I want to go on stage and sing and this kind of stuff. I never really did that. I had been teaching hula since I was 16 years old. My hula teacher gave me her classes to teach, she inducted me into the world of teaching hula. I did not even think I would end up being a hula teacher, ta-da here I am! Hula includes singing, chanting, drumming, and strumming. My teachers made sure that I came into their community very well equipped. It was different back then, it's not like today where we got so many hālaus with kumu hulas popping up all over, it wasn't like that before.

It was very special back then. These teachers made sure you had an arsenal of mele and they made sure you knew what you were doing. Singing and all of that came hand in hand with what I was doing as a hula teacher. I also belonged to a group when I was a teenager called Nā Mele o Papakōlea and I was seventeen or eighteen. We were all the same age or maybe a little older than me, but I taught all these musicians and singers hula and we went out performing. We were performing and I met Mrs. Margaret Osteen, who was a professional musician, singer, and hula teacher in her younger years. She had an upright bass and that upright bass fascinated me. So as a child I would pick it up and play with it, so I became self-taught with the upright bass. That's how I became the upright bassist for Nā Mele o Papakōlea.

In those years upright bass players were far and few between, especially if you sang too. Upright bass players were not singers in those days. So people would call me and ask if I would play the upright bass with them. I would go and it kind of eased me into going and playing music out with different groups. Later a group of cousins and friends were getting together and asked me to play 'ukulele, so we slammed a group together and it was like my introduction to being the lead of a group rather than a bass playa on the side. When I was a bass player I also played with Liam and his group Kaleo o Kalani Trio at the Midway Bar on Thursdays. That's how I got to playing at Shindig Bar in Chinatown on the corner of Maunakea and Pauahi on Fridays. And then I was playing 'ukulele in the lead and I took my group into Sir John's which was on Auwahi St. I don't think it's there anymore, the place changed so damn much. It used to be behind the KITV studio on Ala Moana Blvd.

After that I went back into Kalihi and play music at Pōhaku's on the corner of Nimitz and Mokauea. That was the Hawaiian music capital of the world back then. It was sort of a big deal to be at Pōhaku's, amongst your own people doing their own kind of music. Hawaiian music entertainment is so different now, it really is. I stayed in Kalihi, played at the Pumehana Lounge. This is going to be the middle of the 1970s. I also played for many hula studios, for decades. I had a wide vast repertoire of hula songs. I think growing up with all those older Hawaiians I learned a lot of things and later during my musical career I was often the youngest member in the group even though I was a leader. The other musicians were older and more seasoned, they really knew what they were doing, I felt I wasn't going to learn anything about anybody my age or younger.

Hawaiian Clubs

You know in Hawaiian, we have the pronoun 'o ia, which means he, she, or it. I think amongst the Hawaiian community it doesn't matter what the hell you are. It just didn't matter. Especially when I played music down Chinatown in the Shindig Bar. The people that would come to hear us sing, they would come from Honolulu Harbor. They were Hawaiian Stevedores and you had just other people that wanted to hear Hawaiian music. They would go to the Kukui Market next door, maybe buy some char siu or whatever, roast pork, come to the bar, just slam it on the table, throw their money on a pile and have a good time. They didn't care who anybody was. Even in downtown, you know you had the drag queens, you had everything downtown. People just took people for people. We really didn't have that kind of discrimination. Even when I went into Kalihi, it was still that kind of attitude. They don't care I māhū, they don't care who the hell you are, which was quite wonderful. Nobody really put you down for being yourself. If they put you down, it was okay. When I was playing at Pōhaku's we'd be on the stage singing and the stage was on the Nimitz side, so our backs are facing Nimitz. And then we had a back entrance and I think that's Republic Street. I forget what street it is now and that's where people usually park their car and they came in that back door. Once in a while Sam Nae'ole would come flying in through that door. He was the loudest māhū you ever saw. We would just smile or give a little chuckle and it's not because Sam was māhū, it's because his hair was unkempt and everything else. You know, it was like that. Later on, in the very late 1970s, I'm going to end up at the Blowhole Lounge, which is on Kapahulu

Avenue. This was a very interesting place, the lounge was owned by Mr. Sam Lum, he must be dead by now. It used to be the old Clouds, the building is still there. Today there's an ABC drugstore downstairs, it's by the Queen Kapiʻolani Hotel. The ABC drugstore only occupies a part of what used to be the Blowhole Lounge, 'cause the lounge extended all the way in the back and around the back of the building because there was a jacuzzi and stuff in the back. It was a really beautiful place. Now when I first started in the 1960s the place was called The Clouds and on every floor in that building, there was some sort of entertainment and a separate bar on each floor. Even Maya Angelou sang at The Clouds. It was that kind of place. All kinds of entertainment. It was where entertainers would go for entertainment. That was true of the places in downtown and Kalihi too. Every now and then the entertainers would come out slumming, because they want to hear our music and the stuff we sang.

The Clouds eventually closed, but Sam Lum is going to keep the Blowhole downstairs club. If you walk down Kapahulu Avenue, you would completely walk past it. There was no sign on the sidewalk, not even a window! It was just a door on the sidewalk. When you opened the door you went through this hallway, this dark hallway with only overhead recess lights every so many feet. Then you came to another door and when you opened the door, the stage was on the right, the bar was on the left and it was very tastefully decorated. It was known as, I guess it could be called a gentleman's club. Some people even came in there dressed in suits. You know, nice, nice people. I sang there mainly Hawaiian music. Once in a while Ed Kenny would pop in, other people like Kawai Cockett. You know when people wanted Hawaiian music. We were like entertainers of entertainers.

It was a nice interesting mix of people. It was interesting for those who did not know that place existed, you would walk right past it. There's a reason for that. It's because on Kapahulu and in Waikīkī, the attitude towards gay men is going to change. Not everybody is going to be accepting like in downtown or in Kalihi. That's why they kept it like that, one door, no sign. There were some people who were curious, 'cause y'know I'm on the stage and the door is right to my left, that wanted to know what the hell is beyond this door. They would come to the second door by the stage I just be playing and then I would look around and they'd be gone, only got men in here!

Downtown and Kalihi were local places with local people. You got into Waikīkī you going to have a mix of tourists, visitors, people from other cultures. In the Blowhole, we would get local people in there too and also haoles would come. But everyone in the bar was accepting, there wasn't a problem. It was outside the bar that might have been a problem.

I was also in Polynesian shows in Waikīkī. I was in the Tahiti's Bora Bora, when I was very young. Eighteen or nineteen. Even in high school I was going to be in Kealoha Kalama's Polynesian Review. I also go dancing with Pauline Kekahuna and then at the 'Ilikai Hotel. I was also in this short-lived show at the Reef Hotel, Falaniko's Polynesian Revue. I think the people in the shows were local people, so they didn't make a big deal out of māhūs or anybody. But it's your audience that might, but we don't mingle with the audience anyway.

Glades

In the 1970s downtown was vital and bustling. I mean even the Glades was open. Downtown was busy. I felt safer in downtown than I did in Waikīkī because these people were locals, they kind of took care of each other too. I used to see my friend Melissa sometimes she's all strung out and found in front of the Sam's bar on the sidewalk, so I call the cab, have them take her home. It was like that.

When I started out, I didn't even know a gay bar existed. Because I was with the kūpunas and all this kind, I never knew drag queens existed. I never knew until I went to work at the Shindig Bar and that's when I saw drag queens and māhūs larger than life. Not only drag queens, even Joe Pā'ao'ao when he came work. He came from Nānākuli and he had these big jumbo rollahs in his hair. He also carried a train case and his 'ukulele, getting off the bus, wobbling up Maunakea St. One time I seen a haole call him names from across the street. Joe dropped his train case and his 'ukulele went across the street and beat that haole up to a bloody pulp. I saw it, I thought it was so funny. When Joe was done, he just left that bloody mess there on the curb, came back and picked up his things, came in the Shindig, took his curlers off, teased his hair, got his aqua net, sprayed his hair, and then got ready for the show. It was so wonderful.

One time I was taking a smoke outside the Shindig Bar and these māhūs saw this car going round and round the block and teasing them. I saw a dozen drag queens on the corner of Pauahi, Maunakea, stop this car. Literally grabbed these guys from the windows, beat um up, buss up the car, everything. It was remarkable! This was the first time I really got to know this segment of the population, when I actually worked downtown. I had no clue. The first time I stepped into the Blowhole, I didn't even know bars like this existed. I had a guitar player that was running the lū'au show at the Ala Moana Hotel. I was twenty-one doing all this stuff. He told me to meet him at the Blowhole so I can pay him for his guitar playing. I am thinking, all the way over there? I was thinking about at like Hanauma Bay. He meant the bar! He told me where to go. I see Willy sitting at the bar, we are talking, he asks me to have a drink. I did not mean to stay, but I said okay. Those days I drank whiskey on the rocks. I looked around and I saw only guys in there, guys dancing. I was shocked, I did not know a place like this existed. This is nifty. So you know, even in the '70s things were very secretive. You didn't see people prancing all over the place like you do today. If somebody pranced like little Joe coming up Maunakea Street, you better make sure you know how to kill a person with your bare hands.

The military was discouraged from going to Chinatown and the Glades was off-limits. Sometimes the MP would come to check. In the Glades people would look out for one another. If there was an MP presence, people would be alerted in places like the Glades, someone would yell, "MPs are here!" and they would take the military guys through other doors and exits and lead them down other alleyways. Downtown there is an interesting network of alleyways and secret places, you could get people lost. They would look after and take care of one another. I remember when I was at the Blowhole, I think one of the best times in my life I ever had was when the Royal Canadian Navy came in. I think they were part of RIMPAC. There were dozens of them and they just came in. We all had such a good time with the Royal Canadian Navy in the Blowhole.

They came in uniform. I think they just came in and was like, what the hell are we doing, this is kind of fun, let's just roll with it! I have people that would come from like Tripler and they were in the military and they would come to the Blowhole. We knew they were military and I guess it was alright for them to come. Also they used to publish in the back of the newspaper when certain ships were in town. We used to watch the back of the newspaper so when we knew Pearl Harbor was going to be busy, we were going to be busy. We kind of braced ourselves for that kind of action. There's an element in the military that it's not local, but they wanted to come to the Glades or the Blowhole and wanted to see what's happening. Of course there's gays in the military, always was and always will. It was really fun.

The Glades was a huge dinner showroom. It had three stages. It was that fabulous. It was an actual showroom with dinner tables and everything, like in the movies. The performers at Glades were multi-talented, they could sing, live singing, not lip syncing, dancing. Prince Hanalei, gosh you couldn't touch him, no one could touch what he did. Twirling tassels on his nipples, and his ass, standing on his head and doing it independently. He was fire. Even when he was being contracted for private parties I used to bring my trio in and do the cocktail hour kind of music before Prince Hanalei's show. He was a fantastic entertainer, fantastic human being. The Glades offered you first-class world and literally first-world entertainment. Literally a lot of the entertainers went to other cities like

Chicago, New York, San Francisco, to do their Glades show. It was the kind of prominence the Glades had.

This was in the '70s, very early '80s. Eventually I think the owner of the Glades retired. She had to give up the nightclub. Many of the performers went into other jobs, telemarketing stuff like that. Some moved to the mainland, more than some. They pursued other occupations and lives. It was kind of sad. I think when the Glades started to dismantle was when Wo Fat goes out of business. Downtown slowly morphs. I know the Shindig Bar is now River of Life or something like that. It just fizzled out, kind of sad. Tintin Chopsuey, it's closed, a swing pub, people stopped coming. It might have got shut down by the Board of Health, but damn their food was 'ono!

I think Sam Lum got very old. Then he decided to close up operations. I think it was easier for him to collect rent because he owned the whole building. So, the hell with it, he was done. He got new tenants, the ABC store was easy, so that kind of stuff.

Back to School

It was an interesting time in life because I left college in 1975. After two years I realized I didn't enjoy it. I never really liked school. So I left and worked at the Hotel Waikīkī and enjoyed it. I became the head front desk clerk and senior cashier at the hotel. Then I worked for Hawaiian Airlines for a little stint. Then I worked for Hawaiian Island Tours. Just that kind of stuff for several years and then it occurred to me in 1984 that I should go and finish up college. I started it, damn it I should finish it. By the time I go back, Honolulu Community College is even kind of different. I liked going to school this time. I saw a lot of people I knew from before going back to school too.

I got involved with college life. I joined the Hawaiian Club and became president and vice president of the Polynesian Club. I belonged to all these clubs and I like school now! When it was time for me to graduate with my AA, the counselor said, "Eh you get 86 transferable credits." I said, "What the hell does that mean?" He said, "Well you got 86 credits that UH Mānoa will take from you." I was shocked it was that much. He told me I only needed 124 for bachelor's, so I went and I liked it up at UH Mānoa too. I made new friends, the whole vibe. At the same time I was still singing and teaching hula, I was still doing it all. When it came time to graduate the counselor said, "Eh all you need is 6 credits and you get a professional diploma" and that I knocked it out in a summer. And then after that they said, "Eh all you need is 15 credits for a master's" so I kept going. It was a wonderful journey. Then I decided, I'm going to go to Molokaʻi because I have family there. I love Molokaʻi.

Molokaʻi you either hate or you love it. I went to Molokaʻi to teach school and I loved it. I eventually came back to work at Washington Intermediate School. Then the College of Education tapped me to train student teachers. I was surprised because I just started, but they wanted me to do it, so I became certified. I did this for like eight or nine years. I enjoyed it. I never made any plans about what I wanted to be. I'm not one of those. I just keep going until another road is shown to me. That's how I went into the community college, HCC and then Punahou and ta-da. I'm here. That's kind of how it is.

AIDS

I was on Molokaʻi when Prince Hanalei, the Glades performer, came to live on Molokaʻi with Moana Dudoit. Moana Dudoit was so beautiful. She took care of everybody. She took care of Molokaʻi. Prince Hanalei came to live with her and come find out he had AIDS. We didn't quite know what it was at that time. He died when he was on Molokaʻi. When I come back to Honolulu, I'm going to be a bass player for the Kealoha Kalama's trio. That's when we hear people were so frightened with AIDS. Someone who played music with us, he didn't know he had it. He was getting lumps on his skin and thought it was the soap he was using. He finally went to the doctors and they said you have AIDS. He went into shock, we were all like, this is hitting home. Subsequently I knew about a handful of people who died from AIDS.

People were afraid of AIDS and were scapegoating the gay community. I think the ones that took the hit were drag queens. They were on the front line of it for obvious reasons. You can tell a drag queen, sometimes. People assumed they had it. I had a front row seat to it. Seeing other people in the community and not really understanding and just being careful by reading the literature and being careful. It was not addressed in the hula community, people didn't understand what it was.

Same-Sex Marriage and Becoming a Keaulana

When it was happening, I was like thank god it's finally happening. Keaulana was not the name I was born with, it's a surname. It was Joe Keaulana's name. Joe Keaulana I'm going to meet in 1987, when I get back from Molokaʻi. He's another musician and Joe was married. His marriage was over before we met. I think he was waiting for his kids to get older. When we met, we found out we liked each other, and then we really liked each other, and really really liked each other. When his daughter turned eighteen, he got a divorce and we decided to really be together, so I legally took his last name.

This was before all the marriage stuff. I was born Alama, that's now my middle name. That's how Keaulana becomes my last name. Joe Keaulana was a classic profile of a Hawaiian with high blood pressure, diabetes, classic, classic, whatever the Hawaiians get, Joe had. He worked for Foremost, for most his life, delivering everything else. That's how he had a heart attack, so he had to retire early. He was going through health issues and crap. I got Joe onto my HMSA because of the reciprocal beneficiary and so that's how we did it. I think if there was same-sex marriage then, we would have gotten married. We lived together for so damn long. His mother loved and adored me. His family liked me a lot, his kids and grandkids, even his ex-wife. She of course was upset when it first happened. I talked with her once and told her that I will always respect her because she was the mother of Joe's kids. I think that made things better. Whenever the grandkids need help, you help, you become extended family. You know you marry into someone's family, hell they your family too. You no can say I only married you. That's bs, you married the whole damn family. That's how it works.

The thing is that there are so many Alamas and I was Alama forever and ten days. Get my aunties, my auntie's aunty, and everybody else. I never really learned anything from my family in hula, music, or anything. I been Kimo Alama for a long time, I think Kimo Keaulana sounds nice. I told Joe, I am taking you into my life, your kids, your ex-wife, your mothers, your brothers, your sisters, your cousins, your nieces and nephews, I wouldn't mind taking your last name. His whole family actually thought it was a great idea. I told him I would not purposely bring shame to your last name, if anything I wanted to make it better. So that's it. I said, "This is it, you are my life, so why not?" Get plenty Alamas running around, I don't care. That was one of the closest things you could get to a marriage, taking a last name. In those days we didn't have it. But everybody knew about me and Joe. At first a lot of people didn't believe me and then I would whip out my license and show them the name and shut it down. People couldn't wrap their heads around it. I would tell everybody, "That's your problem, not mine! Get over it because I did."

And so when same-sex marriage was happening I went to the capitol because I knew it was going to be historic. If this had been Joe's lifetime, we would have gotten married. I live in his house now in Nānākuli because I helped Joe get it. He wanted to leave it to me when he died but I told him to give it to his kids, but he felt they wouldn't take care of it. So I got this home because it got started with Joe and myself. When the marriages were first being performed, I think it was at the Sheraton, I was invited too. It was like at 12 midnight, but nah, I'm not going. I was there in spirit. It was something long overdue, way overdue.

6

Aunty Kim Haʻupu
Resistant Beyond Words

I was born at Kapiʻolani Hospital April 20, 1949, in Honolulu. At the time we lived in Kaimukī. I grew up briefly in Pearl City, but my parents decided to move to California, where we lived from 1950 to 1960. We lived all over California, Hayward, Oakland, east, west, north, south, we lived there for ten years. When we came back in 1960 we moved to ʻEwa Beach. We lived at our grandparents' for about six months. My parents were reconciling their marriage so they left us with our grandparents. My grandparents were very interesting. My grandfather would say I was his granddaughter and I would laugh. They knew where I was going before I even knew I was evolving to be and they were very accepting Filipino grandparents. Shortly after my parents got together we moved, I think in the late 1960s to Nānākuli, Waiʻanae. ʻEwa Beach was more populated, but Waiʻanae was just some houses and bushes. It was not as developed.

    I went to Nānāikapono Elementary. When I got there I was a fifth grader and unbeknownst to me I was wearing girl blouses to school. I had no idea girls' blouses had buttons on the left and the boys' were on the right. I would be going to school and my classmates would know I was different. I was kind of feminine and they would be calling me sissy, tilly, māhū, sissy-alice. There was no beating up at that time, that would come later. After seventh grade we went to Waiʻanae High School where I met māhū sisters who were already there in their senior year. They made their entry before me and we were very loud. We were all coming out of our shells, they already knew what I was going to be when they saw me. It was like, "Girl! Welcome to the sisterhood!" They made things okay. The boys weren't good if you were māhū, they were really brutal growing up. Once you were in eleventh or twelfth grade you were safe because you were masters of the high school, but talk about bullying, it was happening way back then. The struggle became more real because wanting to be a woman became harder. You weren't accepted by either boys or girls. Hanging around with someone like us was questioned. It was hard for me. I dropped out in ninth grade, the bullying, it was too overwhelming. I was timid and there was this big conflict going on inside of me. When I went back in eleventh grade, I was more prepared for it. Staying home was not good either because my parents were not supportive of who I was going to become, not at all. They were devout Catholics and my father was a police officer. I was an embarrassment to them, they actually used the word "abomination." I had to look it up actually and I am not that word! I became a thorn in their side because I was so resistant, beyond words!

When I went back to school in eleventh grade, it couldn't have been worse than being at home. I went back and had to repeat some, but I graduated in 1969. There was no adult education at the time, otherwise I would have taken that option. I was happy to just finish it. My parents kicked me out when I was seventeen, prior to graduation. They could no longer stomach me. I went to live with my uncle and aunty in Nānākuli my senior year. I will always love them for taking me in. My journey continued and I lived on the streets with my other māhū sisters. I survived it.

Finding My Niche

One day I was approached by this Samoan gentleman who worked at vocational rehab. I was working the streets and when someone pulls up to you in a car and I think, oh they're looking for a date. But, he pulled up and said he had something better to offer me. I get in and I figure he is just a John. He asked me why I was doing this and we were just talking. He then says that he has something better to offer me so I don't have to live on the streets. I told him honestly, what is there for māhūs? He explained that he was from vocational rehab and he said he could help young boys, young men like me, who are soft, who could maybe go into cosmetology, become a floral designer. I told him I had to think about it and he said he would come back and meet me again. I shrugged it off like it was nothing.

He came back the following day and I was like, who is this guy and why is he doing this? I was very distrustful. I had so much doubt because my family and the people I am supposed to trust didn't want me. He was persistent, so I figured why not? I really didn't have anything to lose. The streets were okay, it offered me something better than my family. I didn't know where I was going.

The Glades were on the streets at that time also, so it was a safe haven for all of us. I didn't frequent there until later when I got my life together and found my niche in the world. So I went to beauty school and he followed me throughout the whole thing. They paid for my college, they gave me a stipend to live. I found a little apartment and rent was like hundred dollars.

It gave me direction. I went to Hollywood Beauty College at Ala Moana Shopping Center and it is no longer there of course. I went and dropped out at first, it felt too slow, so I was back on the streets. But this man was consistent, he came looking for me again. He was not going to give up on me, even at times I was giving up on myself. He followed me through and it took two years, but I finished beauty school. He was with me the whole time, perhaps the only person that showed care for me at that time. Vocational rehab did so much for me and he gave me good direction, he came to the graduation. I no longer connected with my family and I made a promise to myself when my parents kicked me out that I was going to show them. I was going to make myself become who I am meant to be without ʻohana support. And I really did it.

I had my other māhū sisters on the Waiʻanae Coast that were there, but I think all of our journeys are alone. Most of the time you have to go alone with a support network. By the time I finished school I had jobs waiting for me already. The school set you up. I worked at the military base, Barber's Point. I liked this evolution of myself doing hair. I found my niche.

I never went back to the streets 'cause I reached a goal of becoming a cosmetologist. Worked at Crown Waipahu, at many salons. In 1973 I was approached by one of my good Navy sisters that asked me to come work in Waiʻanae. Even though I was from there, I never thought I would live there again, but I did and ended up managing a salon there for forty years. I never kept in touch with the guy that helped me, he went on to help others. I advocated for vocational rehab to the other girls because I was able to get a career there. A good career, vocational rehab was really good to me.

Glades

After I got set in my career I went back to the Glades because I recognized this is my community and I wanted to patronize the Glades and see what it was about. The Glades was the fine art of female impersonation with some iconic performers—Brandy Lee, Ardina Jacobs, who performs in Chicago today, Charmaine Lee Anderson, they were our older mentors. Prince Hanalei was Hawaiʻi's only male exotic dancer, there will be no other. He was from the Waiʻanae Coast. Handsome gentleman, no other like him!

It was a safe haven for many of us who came from broken homes, who came from broken family environments who did not accept our journey of becoming who we were meant to be, to be a woman, or māhū. Without a support network, Glades was the place to be, a safe place and Mommy Aggie was the owner. She helped us, gave us jobs there. I went there with my other sisters to support the Glades and knowing who I had become and being comfortable in my skin, it was good to learn more about the world that I actually come from, which at that time was māhūs and today I am part of the bigger LGBTQ community. This is a worldwide, nationwide community.

We would all share our stories there, share our journeys. Some girls had accepting families, but for those of us who didn't, we were able to be a support network to cry if we needed to, be angry, be mad—and to be what families should be if they throw you out. We were able to talk about that and let go of some of that pain that can seep into you and screw you up. Talking about it is a way to forgive and move on.

Finding Love

Being from the Waiʻanae Coast and then working there, I just wanted to have my job and make a career and move forward, get my gender reassignment, which is what they called it at the time. That was one of my goals. Finding love, to me, was difficult when you are māhū, especially here in the islands. It's interesting 'cause we have different tastes. I was always interested in Black and Japanese, but White and locals were not on my list. Locals always make fun, but you know they would call you in the night. Blacks were cool, very accepting. Many were my friends and some were my boyfriends. I eventually married a local man, so funny to me falling in love with a local man. He was a short very dark gentleman, not handsome. Interesting, but not handsome.

I met him working in a bar on the Waiʻanae Coast. RJs was a straight bar and none of us were even allowed in at the time. It was a fine dining restaurant owned by the Joseph family, who I knew very well. When I was asked if I wanted to work there, I wanted them to know that I am a hairdresser not a waitress and that I am māhū. The owner said it didn't matter, but I said, "It does matter" but I met up with them and they liked me. Even though I did not know how to work bar, they taught me and I went to work. When I went to work I was told to dress however I wanted. I was 150 lbs., long blonde hair and I went in and when I got there, the bartenders gave me attitude! I explained that the Mr. Joseph Rodney hired me and that was it. I worked there for seven years. I would do hair in the morning and then tended bar, was a waitress in the evening. I made good tips. The bar eventually closed of course. I went back to doing hair. I have always worked.

I met my husband there. He came to the bar with his dad. I always made it a habit if men were interested in me to say, "Braddah, I'm māhū, k" and guys were curious like . . . "really?" I never lie, see I do not lie about what I am. Plus I was so loud, I was just a loud māhū, you know? Really! It was okay because I am not deceiving anybody. So, he looked at me and introduced himself as Wayne and his dad. I would shake guys' hands, never honi them, unless they were comfortable. I never wanted to make anybody feel uncomfortable. I was serving them, he tells me later, "would you like to go to breakfast?" and here I am holding my tray and

I started laughing... "Breakfast? Sure." He suggested Anna Miller's, and I was like okay. This bar was open from 9 to 4 and we had a cabaret license. Come to 4 o'clock, we are closing the bar and then my girlfriend Jo comes and tells me that this local dude is outside asking for me, saying we are going to breakfast. I said, "Tell him I left" and I sat in the bathroom after we cleaned up our tables. I asked my friend to tell me when he is gone.

I had not seen him for three months. When he came in later he was a whole different person. He was with a whole group of different men. He was an ironworker and he came with all of his friends. They decided to sit in my section and they didn't want to sit anywhere else. They were being difficult, when I asked them what they wanted, they just looked at each other and laughed. I felt like these locals were going to be a problem. I go back to the table several times and they don't order. I asked my friend Jo to do me a favor and work the table because these local guys were pissing me off. Jo goes to try and work the table, but they call back for me to be their waitress.

I muster up all my energy to go to the table. I tell them, "Guys, I am not here to suck any of you off, I am a simple māhū that's working to make a living. You can either order from me or move to the other side." I was trembling when I said that. These ironworkers, they're bigger than me. They laughed and I was nervous, but they ordered and we became friends that night. They were my regulars after that. It was hard to do that. I am not going to mention their names, some of them became union leaders and are my good friends. Later on, they acknowledged that it took balls for me to talk to them like that. I told them, locals always think that māhūs want them, that we always are attracted to them, but I am too good for that. This made them crack up. Wayne, my future husband, was at that table. He acted like he didn't know me, which was kind of good because I didn't want to know any of them other than being my customers.

Once I knew what they were drinking, I told them to just wave their lighter at me. I was super fast and they were generous tippers. I did not know that these men would become my good friends, even now. We get together and mingle sometimes and talk about that time at RJs bar. I worked there for a while but eventually went back to my job in Waiʻanae and over a period of time Wayne and I would run into each other and we started building a relationship. He was formally married, he came from a Mormon family and our relationship became an issue with everybody in his family. It was hard for me because his family was tough to me. They told me it was wrong, but hey, I told them this was a two-way street. If they had a problem, they should talk to their son, their grandson, because we cared for each other. That relationship turned into forty years with him. We were going to do the same-sex marriage, but I lost him to cancer in 2009, but we lived together for forty years.

Aunty Kim Haʻupu (right) and friend win pageant at Chinese Cultural Plaza, 1986. Photo courtesy of Aunty Kim Haʻupu.

The journey to finding love for anybody is hard, for any gender the struggle is real. For māhūs, it might be even greater because of acceptance. Your husband is going, "I'm going with a man?" and this is always in the back of your head. But I was happy and blessed to have a relationship. Do I want one anymore? No. I have two hānai sons. One is in Miami and another is coming home in September.

Ka Uʻi Wahine Dancers

I always told the girls to enjoy your youth, because when you get older you not going look like this. You might, but it just depends. You have to think about the illusion you put out to whoever and I was like that until I got married. Then I got comfortable. When I was young, gosh I was so skinny. I didn't feel beautiful, but I was pretty enough to get by. We created the Ka Uʻi Wahine dancers with completely local boys, again all from Waiʻanae. This was happening between the '70s and the '90s. Some men from the Big Island saw our show and they wanted to know if we wanted to go to the Big Island to do shows for them. Someone from the Kamehameha Men's Glee Club from the Big Island wanted to meet with all the girls, which were all Wai'anae girls with the exception of three girls from Waipahu—Valerie DJ Michaels, Libra Zamore, and, of course, Ms. Fanny Patigan. They were all from Glades also, not going there, but frequented. We met with them at Kelly's Drive-In.

They all flew in from the Big Island because they wanted to meet up. There were seven of us and I was the MC and singer, it was a variety show, comedic act, all of it. I like them because they were very forward in asking us, point blank, if we were streetwalkers. I was like, the girls work, most of the girls worked in home care or case management. They were happy about that. They wanted to know what kind of shows we put on and they wanted rated G for the public.

In the first show, we didn't have any skin showing, it was a variety show—hula dancing, Broadway hits, *Hello Dolly,* you name it, we did it. We sing live to Patsy Cline, Barbra Streisand, Anita Baker. I am the MC. We would go to the Big Island every summer, put on shows for our men's glee club. We would make about 10 grand on Fridays and Saturdays, two shows each and they cover our room, pay us a flat fee of $2,500. I thought that was damn good. They would always buy the food. But, because everybody eats a lot, well let's say, they eat like men, you know. They said, "Kim do you think you guys can pay for your own food?" And I'm like, "Yeah, I know." I said we can pay for our own food 'cause they do eat like kāne. We laughed about it. I told the girls, "Plane fare, get a car, we get a room, they're paying for that, but we just paying for our own food because everybody eats like kāne." And everybody laughed. I said, "Mary, you know that's true okay." We can help them out, it's a flat $2,500 divided by seven of us, it was damn good. We flew back every summer and looked forward to going.

We performed at the Keauhou Beach Hotel, at the Hyatt Waikoloa, the Nani Loa, which was amazing where we performed because it was this big hall. The Nani Loa was like a mini small Vegas, a stage and chairs and like a counter you know. The show was made for tourists and locals and it was amazing. We even performed for Aunty Leilani Mendez for her Mother's Day show in Nānākuli right next to Paradise Cove. She asked us to be part of the show. The crowd was amazing, I told the girls, we would always pule kākou before we start going on stage and give it to them! I was like, give it to the crowd!

Locals are great because they love drag shows. They're our best supporters. Tourists also love it, they have drag shows on the mainland, but they aren't as pretty as the local girls. They do look like truck drivers in wigs. The new girls that are coming out are very pretty, the ones that I have seen on Instagram. We had many performers there, some of the girls have moved on. They moved to Vegas, they're older now, they can't go on stage and carry on.

So we performed for about seven years and we were all working and when we decided to go to Maui or the Big Island, we just take off from our jobs and go off on the weekend and come back on Monday. It was great performing and we kind of like people know that we're out there, the Ka Uʻi Wahine Dancers and Company. We had people in the background to help change, who just wanted to go. We had our own light technician, a production crew that would set up while we were there.

Our second group was the Glades Glamour Girls Debut, the girls of today. We did have two girls that took it all off, not all off, but you know pasties here and there. Beautiful bodies! It was good. Even if we had to cover up, I would tell the girls, we have kūpuna in the audience, we have to be mindful. And we have kids over there. Some of the other girls didn't like it, I said, "Why it's a form of entertainment?" and two girls had pretty bodies and the girls would say, "Are they really boys? 'Cause they don't look like it." As long as you're getting paid don't get J of the next person, you know? I always had to be the mediator because sometimes the girls can get y'know.

We performed at the 4th of July extravaganza held at Sunset Beach. It was a success. Everybody knew that the Glades Glamour Girls were going to be there. It was packed! It was packed from here to across the street, everybody wanting to see them. I always told the girls, we play, and I looked at the girls and said, "This is amazing, everybody is out there to see our show, so give it your best. Sell the show!" And they would go out, we always had an opening number, "Bad Girl" by Donna Summer. We come out and everybody is screaming, like I am in the back nervous because after that I have to go out and welcome everybody to our show. People would be screaming! After I introduced our show and asked, "How do you like our opening number?" they would scream, scream! I said, "I am overwhelmed Waiʻanae!" But the girls wanted me to just introduce their names. You know the gimmick was "Mr. . . . ." and here comes this beauty, but they did not want that. That group lasted about six years. I gave the group to one of my girlfriends. It was a great time, but I was moving on with yet another job within the mental health field, at the State Department of Health.

Being a Caseworker

I went into mental health around 1991. I went to work at our local Waiʻanae mental health at that time as the receptionist. That job turned into four years. I was on call, so I let the girls run the salon. I told the girls, "I am going to be moving into a different career. I am going to leave the comfort of a beauty salon and go work with straight people." The supervisor asked me to work there, she liked my work and I had clerical experience. I became a case manager after four years. It was scary and frightening because again, I had to be accepted by a whole different realm of heterosexual people. Though people knew me, I'm leaving my comfort zone, but I was willing to give it a try. That turned into my next career for 17 years. I worked there for 10. There were obstacles. I didn't want to work with men, I didn't know if they wanted me to be their case manager because I was māhū.

I asked my supervisor if I could just work with women and she said no. She said, "That issue you have is yours." And she was right. I had to formulate if I am going to work with men, how am I going to do this? The simplest way is being honest and open, so when I met with all my men clients, we would go out. I didn't like being at a desk, I liked being outside sitting under a tree. We would talk outside. I would say, "Hello my name is Kim, I'm going to be your new case manager and I just want you to know that at any time you are not comfortable with me we can find you somebody else, I am māhū." The local guys would look at me and tell me, "You local yeah?" I said, "I am." "Then that's all, that's good enough for me. I no like no haole being my case manager." My barrier broke that day. Another wall, all these walls that come up because you're māhū, you know. I exposed myself to a new world that was forthcoming.

Me and my other gentleman friend had the biggest cases, we were only supposed to have 30, we had 40. Most of them were men, they were like hardcore people, dual diagnosis, drugs, and either schizophrenia, bipolar, a combination of both, along with drug addiction. I was like, okay. I had to muster up all my experiences from childhood and bring it forward. That turned into 17 years of really good work. I moved on from a nonprofit into the state department of health, adult mental health. I think I worked there for three years in the clubhouse psychosocial program.

It was really good. The only time I felt barriers was when people from the state hospital would come to visit the program and spend the day with us, interview everybody. They didn't know who was a member or who were the workers. It was interesting because they saw me as a māhū, so they would ask me, "How long have you been coming to this program?" and I would go along with it and tell them that I was there for ten years and that I liked the program. I knew they were judging me, they thought I was a member. One day we are all having lunch together and the director was going to introduce all the staff. When she got to introducing me, the state people had this look on their face, they were so wrecked and embarrassed. They asked why I didn't tell them and I told them they had already thought I was a client. I can see that look on their face. They were embarrassed. That was good learning for me. People always have ideas about māhūs. My boss asked me later why I didn't say anything and I told her, "You know, Linda you not māhū, you'll never know when people look at you the way they look at me. They're already looking at me, knowing what I am and judging me, thinking I am a client. Thinking I have to be a client because māhūs can't work at this kind of program." She understood what I was saying. That day, those people learned that māhūs can work regular jobs and we can move forward. We can face challenges and be as productive as anybody else despite what they think we can or cannot do.

As a case manager, I am kind of like a social worker. We meet with individuals and the first thing I do is make sure you got your benefits, you have lodging, you have food. I work with you to find a place, a temporary shelter. My job is to make sure you remain stable in the community, you work on goals and projects to get you from here to there and to maintain it. Throughout the whole course I am going to be there for you. Independent living is the goal. We try to keep you stable, if you get sick again or depressed or you end up in the hospital again, I am there. I show up as the case manager, "Mary what's going on?" You know it is always with the guys, never the women. I say, "Braddah, what's going on?" They know they were shitty or did something wrong. I would talk to them about getting back on their feet. I not going to fill their ears with what they did wrong. They already know. My job is to get them back stable, be there, get Braddah back together. Boom!

When I left it was hard because I left my clients. When you know people, we all ride high, sometimes we go down, sometimes we're in the middle, we gotta be there. I don't know but what I seen today, case managers aren't as aloha. You have to have aloha and if you from Hawai'i you have a lot of aloha. That makes us, the aloha spirit. We did good working there, everybody to me was like my own 'ohana.

My director would talk about counter-transference and you know, I would tell her that's a white thing, it's not a Hawaiian thing. Hawaiian thing yeah, you love your family, you're there for them, you hear them, you hear their heart. Yeah, you gotta, you might argue but the whole thing is getting them back to love, to aloha. Counter-transference, I didn't know, because every story I hear it has meaning, it's deep. The pain that people go through, I know that pain. I know that pain, okay. I've come through that, they can become better. I don't know how long, the healing is different for everybody, the healing of pain is different. You know, something trigger us back to the ugly times in our lives, that's painful. And when it's painful we resort to . . . drugs, whatever, so you can talk about that.

Wai'anae Coast Kūpuna Council

Recently I got involved with the Kūpuna Council, we just chose the name of an event we are doing, Mana Māhū Extravaganza, to put on the shirt. Everybody wants a drag show you know. My nephew asked us what the show was going to be about, what would be the aftermath of it? Everybody wants a drag show to carry on, but we decided we needed to put together some sort of support network group for keiki that are coming up. They are coming up as we speak. The community is out there and we need to support them. The goal after this show is to work with the Boys and Girls Club, we want to also put it in the schools. Waiʻanae High School, Nānākuli High School, intermediate. I told the Suzuki Foundation, who is going to help, that I didn't want to touch elementary schools because parents get upset. I have met parents that were so upset about their child and I grab the parents' hand and I hold them, I say, "No matter what that is your bebe. You need to love this child. I believe this child is the one that going take care of you." I said, "I come from parents that were not supportive, you cannot be ashamed of this child, whether boy or girl, whatever, this is your bebe. You need to be there for them, you have to, or else they going land up on the street. They might not see adulthood." 'Cause family is a great impact. We need our parents to accept us, we need our parents to validate us.

I tell my friends that. Your child needs you to validate them no matter where they go and if you don't do that then all is lost in their world. Because we talk about roots, family being roots, some of us no more. We grow up creating roots but we don't know if the roots that we going create is good, you know. So our journey is going to end, that's why I need this time because if it becomes a reality, which I know it will, I want to be there.

So we're putting this together, we do have the blessings of the Boys and Girls Club to move on with this. We are just going to be finishing up the letter, using the terminology "All Female Impersonation," because I don't know about drag sometimes gets people worried. I always used the word māhū, I always have 'cause that's what I am. Besides being Kimberly Haʻupu you know. I see "māhū" on Facebook more now. First it was transexual, then transgender and sometimes words break away, but the one word that represents all of them is "māhū." All the words, it is just labeling. But, I am a transwoman, that is my label. I think the world wants to know if you are transgender. I am māhū, but could I use that word in California or Mississippi or in the Deep South? No! If I did, would my life be at risk if they find out what it is? Māhū is great.

7

Manulani Aluli Meyer
ʻAʻohe pau ke ʻike i ka hālau hoʻokahi

My name is Manulani Aluli Meyer. I am the fifth daughter of Emma Aluli and Harry Meyer. We are from the Aluli ʻohana, the Keoʻekai ʻohana, the Naeīhe ʻohana, the Keawaehiku ʻohana, and also the Meyers from Bell Hill, Illinois. I live today in Pālehua, in a home called Waolama, about two thousand feet above sea level. I grew up on the shores of Mōkapu on Oʻahu and in Kailua. We grew up right on the beach at this place called Hoʻomaikaʻi. It was an acre of land that had an old 1924 house. Before that we grew up with all of our cousins: Emmett Aluli, the Aluli ʻohana, we had like five houses altogether and we left in about 1964 when I was five. But I remember Mōkapu and then Kailua, but I like to say I grew up in Hilo, Palikū. My ʻohana is originally from Hilo One. Hilo Palikū is Pāpaʻikou, Kalauomauka, Pepeʻekeʻo, Alia, these are places that had beautiful old, old, funky homes like the one I live in now. I lived there for about thirty years. There are seven siblings in my family, six girls and one boy. Malia, Mele, Maile, Moana, my twin, who is also gay. Luana the younger sister, and Maui, the boy. There are seven of us. Malia has since passed, my eldest.

The Cowgirls (Santa Barbara)

In college, I was a volleyball player. Shoji was my coach in high school. I got recruited to UC Santa Barbara. This is when it started. She was twenty-three years old. Sandy Kegan was captain of the volleyball team and I was eighteen. I didn't know anything. I got to a point where I was frustrated, frustrated that everything in my bones says this is wrong. I couldn't even say the word lesbian, I can't even say it now. I did not think I was gay, I was just in love with this woman. Reminds me of the shirt, "I am not gay but my partner is," I used to really like that. Sandy was the captain for the team, five years older than me! She was not gay either. I don't know what it was, it's like the first dive into your orientation is a dive into this deep attraction. For me it was her mind, and then, you couldn't go anywhere else. Same with her. It was very difficult. Your first one is very difficult to get over.

Everything was private. She was the captain of the team. I am the freshman, you're the blocker, starter. Hello! We were both shocked. We were not out on campus, but there were a group of women that came to our games and they called themselves "The Cowgirls" and they were these twenty-three- and twenty-five-year-old Santa Barbarians that loved volleyball. They came and scooped me up and adopted me. I coached their softball team. I got really close with them and comfortable in bars. I was eighteen, good enough in California. We would hang out in gay bars. I was coach for the Unicorn Softball team, all women. I was thrown into it and loved every minute of it.

Me and Sandy were together for a year and a half. She became bulimic, I think she was really doubting herself. I tried to go with men too. Is this a phase? I was eighteen, nineteen, that is like sinfully young. You try to go with men, but it's like, no. I always say in my heart, once you're with women, oh my god, there is no comparison. It is everything. Being a very body-centric intelligent woman, I felt being with a woman was more natural to me. It was hard to lose my partner when she became bulimic, she had to go into the hospital and her mother took her, I never saw her again. It was hard, but you get over your first one, yeah?

The Cowgirls took me in. I didn't know how to play softball, but they wanted me as a coach. They put me with Sandy Beats, another Sandy. After 30 years, Sandy found me again, and we have become friends. These were motorcycle mama girls, just beautiful surfer and community types. One even became a beloved friend and took me to India 15 years ago. These women really affected me. I was young and they helped me not to be afraid, or not normal. After two years I couldn't play anymore. I got injured, I had five surgeries in a year. My scholarship ran out. I knew coming home would change everything. Santa Barbara was a beautiful, wonderful, beginning. Coming back to Hawai'i was another thing.

Coming Home (O'ahu)

During the interim of coming back, my parents saw Sandy kiss me on the beach in Kailua. My father was watching. He was very angry. I don't know when I had to leave the house, but I was asked to leave. My mom didn't talk to me for about a year. My sister Maile took me in, she and her husband because they were both living in sin because they were not yet married. Catholics! In the '70s you can't even say you're sleeping with your boyfriend at all! Maile was sleeping with her boyfriend, so they were ousted. I was ousted. We were all un-Catholic. I do love the Catholic church though, I love the ritual and the smells. I love God in my own freaky way, but the whole God thing was oppressive. I left the church and found God in my own way. In my Hawaiian way.

Anyway, with bad knees and no support from my family, I just worked and coached volleyball at Kaimukī High School. I worked at Arcadia and a lot of different places, made enough for rent, and went to UH Mānoa. UH was hard. I had a bike and a bum knee and I would bike everywhere on my one knee. If you saw me it was hilarious. I had a cane strapped to my bike and I would push the pedal. Injured athletes are depressed beings. I swear I could make a living facilitating depressed, injured athletes who ultimately become serious alcoholics or abuse other drugs. I was the poster child.

I went to bars bars bars. I am a drinker. I absolutely stopped. It's been a long journey. Both my parents were alcoholics, my brothers and sisters died of alcohol-related illnesses. Kaumaha! My Hawaiian heart is heavy. The sports are just the tip of the iceberg for that, but yeah, I came home when I was twenty-five, after working for Outward Bound. It's interesting, your work allows you to actually know who you are too.

In 1982, my partner at the time, Cheryl Gabel, was in PhD school and she went to Colorado. I followed her and got a Master's in Exercise Physiology. I follow my partners. She was special. Just two years of relationship. My life is relationships, that's what I always say. My relationships are my best teacher. Loving is my best teacher. I stayed there for two years and coached volleyball, track and field. The head volleyball coach was gay and she just adopted me. They call it gaydar and I know my gaydar is good, you just have to be a decent human being I guess. Women help each other. Women helped me along the way. I got my Master's in Colorado and then came to Hilo. I wanted to come home.

Hilo

I was twenty-five when I went to Hilo. I went there because I did not want to shame my family, but even more than that, I loved rain. I just loved Hilo. I rented a car for two days and just drove along the coast where I went to live, Pepeʻekeo side. I found a little sign, "house for rent $200" in 1985. I talked to the landlord and got the house. I was living alone for a while and I loved Hilo. Hilo taught me more of my place in Hawaiʻi. I loved the solitude and the beauty. I knew every waterfall along the Hilo Palikū coast from Wailuku to Alia, to Pepeʻekeo. I used to bring my students down to Kawainui, ʻAwāwaloa, Kalua, all these kinds of secluded waterfall areas. I loved it. I carved stones there. I love solitude, but I was with partners there too. They have beautiful old homes there. It was in Hilo, away from my family, that allowed me to grow.

I wanted to be a wilderness instructor throughout my life. When I came to Hilo, I found my way mystically. David Sing hired me, the only Hawaiian with a

Master's on-island in 1985. He needed a counselor. I also coached with Sharon Peterson for six years, she was the winningest volleyball coach in America, in the NAIA Division I. She was good. I never left sports until I had to. I left for Harvard in 1993. But Hilo is where I call my home of the heart. I grew up there in many ways, as a Hawaiian. My family is Hawaiian, but we were separated from our Aluli cousins, it was very hard.

There weren't too many women in Hilo, I met Polly there she was from Minnesota. She used to be Val Kanuha's partner, she introduced us. We just hit it off. Polly and I were together for almost ten years. She still lives there with Wanda, who is part of the Puna Rude Girls. They were a great group of women who would roll up in their motorcycles, help you fix your house, dig ditches, party til you drop in your bed. I didn't live in Puna, I lived in Hilo Palikū, but Puna was a place you could get an acre and a home for twenty thousand, and a home! Those were fun days, but I didn't want to live in Puna. I'm not Pele. I'm not a Pele clan, I'm a moʻo. Once you get that straight in your naʻau then you know where you going to live, what you going to do, how you going to do um. Hilo Palikū, the place of muliwai, that's where I grew up. Along Onomea, Kawainui, my favorite. Then there was Hanawī liʻiliʻi, Hanawī nui, Kahāliʻi. It has been 12, 15 years since I been those places, but I used to go every week, walk down to those places and it was very helpful.

Beauty educates me. I love beauty. I am a practitioner of many things. My Molokaʻi friend brought me to Buddha, to a different practice. I been a student of Buddha for many years, and Christ, and Rumi, and Baba Muhammad, Yahka Khan, and Aunty Kalaepaki, and ʻIolani Luahine, and "Change we Must," Nana Veary. I like all those women. I am from a plethora of beauty, because if it makes sense, accessorize!

Harvard

My family and friends would ask me why I would go to Harvard if I was interested in Hawaiian philosophy, but there were lots of people there to learn from. I went to Harvard for five years. I was the fastest in my class. I went there to learn from Howard Gardner the bodily-kinesthetic guy, Carol Gilligan, and Larry Goldberg, who wrote *The Moral Inventory*. Carol Gilligan taught me to question the Goldbergs and all these assumptions about how boys and girls think. Gilligan became a mentor, she told me to ignore Howard Gardner. Emmett Aluli would tell me to get out of there, but I felt the need to finish it. I was there for three years and then came home to finish it in Hilo. You can't write about a Hawaiian topic outside of Hawaiʻi because it just becomes a thing of the head. For me it's a thing of the heart. That's why my thesis is published today. Maile made me give it to her, the press wanted it. They wanted to take the word "epistemology" out of it. But I said, "Fuck, don't take the word 'epistemology' out!" They were afraid that people wouldn't understand it, but I felt like, let them suffer!

This was my book, Hoʻoulu. Maile just sent it out, she xeroxed it. That is what siblings do! People would tell me that they had my xeroxed thesis and I had no idea. Maile developed ʻAi Pōhaku Press and then UH Press wanted it. I am not a writer, I just started reading after I got injured. I really don't think I am a writer at all. Maile said, "Well people are reading it." All that mattered to me was that people are reading it, it is affordable, and that it is done by my family. Mele did the art, Maile published it, my twin Moana did one of the forwards. So, nepotism rocks. We are about something different. My work really consumed me, so my orientation was way in the back of the bus. My work stimulates me. In my personal life, my orientation aided in ways that allowed me to understand myself in different ways.

The Efficacy of Aloha

In the search for peace, you find the efficacy of aloha. Once you start to love, there's no telling what we could do with others. That is what I think our kūpuna is all about and that's what ʻike kupuna is all about. I had to go to a fancy high makamaka place and realize it. Sometimes I would be in these rooms with academics and wonder, this shit is supposed to be intelligent? These guys? Oh my god, America is in trouble, but it is now our time to be of service. I mean it. Hoʻokahi lāʻau he mihi. The first medicine is forgiveness, then we can help. It's so shocking to see what's behind the veil because there is nothing there. It is my job to tell people, we are the ones we been waiting for. We are so ʻakamai, it's not even funny. When I bring my people into the room in academia and the room just gets intelligent. You can feel the academics salivating. That's why I am careful about where I bring my beloved people, because there is so much extraction. There is "no social justice without cognitive justice," that's what DeSouza Santos says. That's why I been watching universities collapse in the last fifteen years, because we have to figure it out together.

I had a friend, June Gutmanis, she's a researcher, poʻe haole, lived in Puna, very unusual woman, she put together *Nā Pule Kahiko* and *Lāʻau Lapaʻau*. We became friends and she would say, "Oh Manu, get over it," regarding my gayness. She put the *Journal of Homosexuality*, in 1987 or whatever and when I saw it for the first time I was so shocked! A journal for homosexuality? And an article about Pacific homosexuality? Super freaky! This one article saved my life, that was about naming people like me. There were two articles that saved my life, that one that made me think, I'm not a māhū, but I feel like I'm an aikāne. The article blew me away, like, this is normal?! I learned there were people like aliʻi that were with their own gender, like duh. It made me feel part of culture, that helped me heal. June Gutmanis gave me that article and another article from some freaky spirit magazine, a spirit little book that said, "If you're born gay. You're the lucky ones." I was like what? So in this life, you are on the way out of a cosmological cycle of being birthed and reborn. Now your job is just to focus on what you are meant to do in this lifetime and then you can cycle out. This is what got me really into studies of spirit and spirituality.

The article helped me understand aikāne, the takatāpui in Aotearoa and the faʻafafine in Samoa. You start to see this. When I went to India they're the people blessing the children, the hijras.[1] All of a sudden you start to see yourself in society. Granted, I am not a cross-dresser, although when I wear muʻumuʻu I say I am dressing in drag. You know you gotta wear your muʻumuʻu every now and then. I go, "okay girls, I'm dressing in drag." My sisters roll their eyes, but you know, my sister Moana says, "paint it red." I love wearing those special muʻumuʻu, the light collar, just old-fashioned. You paint it red. The aikāne article changed my life because it gave me historical context to my person. Then I got to be able to move through it, you know, just keep moving. It was an obstacle and then it became a companion and then it became a friend and then it became part of my recipe to leak. This is not who you are, this is what you think you are. That distinction allowed me to get to the next chapter in my life. Which is what our people did, you know what I mean. Meaning, we lived in a way that was true to ourselves. It wasn't anti-anything, it wasn't pro-anything. It wasn't fuck you, it wasn't angry, it was just normalized. It was a normalized way of being. And when I realized that this is a state of my own evolution, no need brag to get to what that evolution is pointing to. I learned a lot from these articles.

When you start to see the trauma in others, you feel kaumaha for them and you try to help them in ways you can. I started saying in my classes, because I taught Intro to Education, I said, "Okay, guys, I'm only going to say it once . . ." to my 100 students or whatever, "when you find students in your class that are gay or you think that they are, you can't come up to them and say that it is choice." You could see everyone in the room go like, what? I would tell them, "It's not a choice, it's an orientation." I would make everybody say it. The room would become uncomfortable. That was the closest I got to coming out. I would say, "It's

---

1. Referring to eunuch, intersex, trans, or third gender people in the Indian subcontinent.

an orientation. Got it, everybody?" You could tell there were whispers. That was the closest I ever came to coming out.

Homophobia in the Lāhui

I remember there were prominent people in the Hawaiian community who were very anti-gay, very negative. Nobody would come up to me, this was the '80s, early '90s. People were interested in Hawaiian culture and what that meant. You know what they say in the Hawaiian community, "You can go ahead and be that, but hoʻoulu lāhui."

I had my own way of learning and that's alright. I raise my children with ideas. Not everyone is supposed to have children. I found that in the aikāne article. That was honorable. We took care of children, we took care of genealogy, we took care of star knowledge, we took care of philosophical knowledge, we took care of things like that. I appreciated that 'cause it helped me get on my path. Hawaiian culture helped me get out of my self-doubt. It really did and then it was also the prison, 'cause you know in the '80s, Hawaiians were very homophobic. Māhūs in hula were tolerated because of their fantastic creativity, but not women. Honestly, not women. I don't care what people say about Hawaiians, I know in my own community, it was hard. I told them that when I left for Aoteaora.

Hawaiian society can be very religious. It was complicated. It was the '80s man, we were all homophobic. Everyone was in the closet in Hilo, so we were kind of an unhealthy bunch in this way. We did not accept people. I would have loved to sit down and talk to the more famous ʻōlelo people who were gay but not out, but that was not going to happen. We didn't see each other in these ways, at all. I didn't learn ʻōlelo from them for these reasons. It's a long story. Ke noʻonoʻo nei au i kēia manawa. I learned in my own time. They were homophobic to the max. You know it, I know it.

This is why we gravitate toward other races, cultures, people. You know that is what catapulted me into a universal look at life and the specificity that I can drill down into the depth of a specific practice, idea, or hoʻoponopono, whatever it was. I'm a haku. Boom. Then you bus out to universal principles. Don't tell me Hawaiian is better than others, and fuck you for saying that. Separate yourself from what separates you from others. I learned the hard way that Hawaiian culture is brutal. You guys going be brutal? Okay good, I am going to be a Hawaiian doing my thing over there and you guys go over there. You do your thing. I wasn't comfortable in my skin with being how do you call, a hapa like this. I would have left Hawaiʻi long ago like my twin sister did. My twin sister is real brown brown

Hawaiian looking. I stayed here but she's in Portland, Oregon. That stuff does shape you.

I remember 1983 before I left for Colorado I was giving a talk at the UH medical school. There were like fifty people in the auditorium and I was scared shitless, but all they wanted me to do is answer questions. And I remember the biggest questions was which psychiatrist do I go to. You fuckin kidding me? You guys think I'm sick? It is in the DSM IV as an illness. It was in my sociology books as an illness. I didn't see myself as ill, but everybody else did. Fuck off and just let me try not to kill myself, like many of my friends. I stopped counting after fifteen or twenty. Not all on this issue, but the majority on this issue. We survived, barely.

When I lived in Hilo one of our beloved, beloved dancers died of AIDS. I forget his name now, but he was a tall American local boy, my god it was so hard no one would talk about it. I remember thinking, holy shit it's here! I was not in Oʻahu where it was more active and the girls were not affected as much. We were shell-shocked in Hilo. He was a good gentle soul. AIDS was not as much an issue in Hilo. I knew in the hālaus they were stamping it out. I would hear horror stories about someone who just got ʻūniki'd in a hālau but then got injured and people thought they shouldn't have ʻūniki'd him. It was the first ʻūniki in thirty years. They thought he got injured because he was gay because they were so homophobic. Some prominent Hawaiians would publicly talk about how you can't be gay kind of thing and I was so bummed because I wanted to learn. I was so worried to be found out, so I just kind of bleed into the background. Hilo was both liberating and oppressive. Liberating in my heart and my oppressive in this physical form.

Aotearoa—The Time of Love

My sister died and made me promise her that I would let myself be led. So I'm standing somewhere doing this evaluation thing and there's this woman holding *Hoʻoulu*. Turns out it was Linda Tuhiwai Smith. I gasped! Malia told me just be led. Linda invited me there in 2003 and then I went back in 2005–2010. I wondered why I was meeting her and she told me that I am supposed to go to Aotearoa on sabbatical. So I went and I met Ngahiraka. She's a senior curator for the entire country for Māori Art. My sister told me to meet her and I was just happy not to meet anybody but that was 18 years ago. I lived there for six years, and then five other years and worked at the Te Wānanga o Aoteaora, the Maori university with 35,000 students. I developed their only Master's program in Applied Indigenous Knowledge, called He Waka Hiringa. It was a blast! But I'm so glad to be home. We not Māori.

They were just so ritual and giving. We got something else happening here. I see our dysfunction but completely see our function. We get the aloha spirit, we get something else. We get the Hina, they get the Kū. Aotearoa was very healing to me. When you walk in with Ngahiraka Mason, she's her family. Her sister wrote the Māori dictionary, in Māori. She's the first Māori curator, national and international renowned. I walk in there and everyone knows, so that helped. It opened doors. Te Wānanga o Aotearoa is like an enlightened college, the largest cultural experiment in high education in the world. We worked with people nobody else wanted. I loved working there. There's some people like me, you know, so what if you're a dyke? What else? Are you a carver? Are you a lāʻau lapaʻau? Are you kapa haka? Somehow it's more accepted over there. I got that stereotype, it felt like that. The CEO asked me to come, and when the CEO comes in, he was a wonderful Māori gentleman and his wife is a good friend. You know we are all friends. They did not have an issue with being gay and they loved Ngahiraka. She became one of the teachers in the Master's program, her and her sister, and that saved the program. We have the two best people in the country, in this Wānanga. Wānanga is this Māori university. They really upped the game.

I totally saw a lot of māhū and they had their place in how they sat people, how they were weavers, a lot of weavers. It felt more acceptable. I was fifty years old and I was a different age. You see things differently when you age. You tolerated things differently, you feel things differently and in Aotearoa it felt like Māori were more accepting, this is from my direct experience.

When I was in Rarotonga watching kupuna kālai waʻa, he had a poem book and gave it to me. I read it, said, "Te aroa, te aroa, te aroa" which means love. Like, te aloha, te aloha, te aloha. I go "Uncle, te aroa means love?" So isn't Aotearoa the time of love? And he goes, "Yeah." I go, "Why don't Māoris know that?" He responded, "You tell me." So I come back to Aotearoa, I go, "Eh you guys, you know what Aotearoa means? You think it's the land of the long white cloud, but it also means a time of loving." And all these burly guys, with mokos on are like, "Wow I like that." I go, "Yeah, a Hawaiian taught you that." Because aloha is our intelligence. That's what I learned. In Aotearoa, I learned about living here. So take that, and work on it and know that your Hawaiian cousins, give this to you. They are beloved. But I had to come home. So yeah, I think we get it here. That's what I learned in Aotearoa, we have it here.

Marriage

We got married, we got married twice. First we did a Hawaiian style at Ulupō heiau. Ty Kāwika Tengan did the ʻawa bowl. Keawe Kaholokula was one of the kiaʻi

Manulani Aluli Meyer (left) and Ngahiraka Meretuahiahi Mason. Courtesy of Manulani Aluli Meyer.

and my nephew Kapono. They did the ʻawa bowl and then it started to rain and filled the ʻawa bowl, it was really mythic. We did it right before as an energy to help, energetically, kūkulu kumuhana, push it forward. I was in Aotearoa when it happened and I saw marriage pass, it was really kind of mythic it made me cry like wow! You can get fuckin married? I was still shy but then I finally did it officially here in Hawaiʻi. You go into the place and you know they ask where is your husband? And I'm like she's over there. So same thing everywhere I go. I go with Ngahiraka now to her appointments and they ask, "Where's your husband's insurance card?" It's my wife, I go, "Howzit you guys?" I'm out, I'm out! It really helped me. Now I say I'm gay. Before I didn't. Sixty-three years old before I did it. The nurse called me when she was in the hospital and I explained I'm her partner, her wife. I used the W word. "You have to call me." And they did. If I wasn't they wouldn't have. I knew my rights but I wanted to remind them. In an ʻoluʻolu kind of way. Because this is who she has. That's me, call me, okay, "I'm her wife. Everybody on this floor, okay?" If I didn't, if I wasn't married, I couldn't assert that. They would ignore it. Maybe I don't know what they would say before, "Are you her friend?" Family only. I have heard horror stories from friends whose beloveds died and they couldn't go in there. Horror stories, so at least that can stop.

When we got married Louisa Wong did it, she was a good friend, she became prime minister. That was amazing. She was a rugby player. The energy in the world is shifting, as the world organizes these issues are going to be less and less important and it's going to cycle into a different way. I can see it. I feel like there is an extreme form of hatred that lessens into tolerance then lessens into witnessing, that poofs into understanding with everything. It's like evolutionary, we are evolving. It happened pretty quickly so the people that are still hanging on to this hatred based on text/scripture they're becoming a minority. And it might take a few generations but they'll be like weaned out because their children's children will be gay. I used to think, like what 17% are gay! I think it's even more now. People don't even know! But it's definitely something more than that. So play the numbers. This type of oppression will leave us because it's important to keep evolving. There will be other conflicts so evolve through and with. Because conflict is that operating force of change, it's what moves the circle the other way. It happened pretty quick. I was amazed. I couldn't quite believe it. Unbelievable!

I did it because I wanted to change the energy and I wanted them to know that our nephews and our nieces and our cousins were valuable. I didn't think gay rights was my issue. I didn't think sovereignty was my issue. Freedom is my issue. I have a different take on the world because of my disciplines. My friends and family fight for freedom for sovereignty and I do *ea*, in Hawaiian, means freedom, it's a different type of freedom. For me kūkulu kumuhana is a practice. That is when you animate a collective energetic field by participating in it in an integral way and that was marrying Ngahiraka. It wasn't technically marrying her it was spiritually marrying her. And showing my family I'm not homophobic around this. So if you guys are, that's your issue. I think I was fifty-five.

'A'ohe pau ke 'ike i ka hālau ho'okahi

Things are changing, we are in a different world now. I feel like a boring gay woman, seeing all these younger people these days. I am in a different kind of interest around the gender issue. I think we are purposed this way for a purpose. We figure it out and let's collectively, emerge. There was this one time five years ago and I was looking around at my life and in my meetings and there was mostly gay women in leadership positions! That's so amazing! It's so amazing to me. Now is an interesting time to talk to women, to be mentored by women, to be encouraged by women, straight or not, but it's just the rise to the feminine is on. That's why I tell people I'm entering my feminine years. Finally it's happening to me!

When you internalize homophobia self-loathing is kind of basic for everybody. My friends kill themselves, my family kills themselves. It's like wake up! Stop it stop it, māhū! It stopped. I don't wave a flag, but I do tell people. I give talks. People keep asking me for mental health talks, so I always kind of slip it in. "By the way, still alive, shouldn't be." You know you try to kill yourself on this issue, absolutely. You just get so fed up with yourself. The internalized self-oppression is serious with gay people. Fuckin serious. I'm glad I'm over that. If you aren't, let me help you out of that box of discomfort, get out of it! How I got out of it, is understanding we are not our bodies. If we think with our bodies then we think we are our sexual orientation. We are not. I understood that cognitively through the Buddha but understand that ʻoiaʻiʻo. Manaʻoʻiʻo through a friend who died. She came back and said, "Oh my god, Manu we are so not our bodies." She explained so now, I get it. So if I'm not my body, then I'm certainly not my orientation. I'm not my race. Not my gender. That's what I believe. Nobody asks me about this because it's too fuckin far out, but for me it's how I live.

I am a freedom fighter, let's live free! Don't need to own anymore. This house is just a rental. I don't own this, forget it! This is a rental that I can afford the rest of my life. We are not going to own. Ownership is the temporary right to exclude. But what can we do? We can kūkulu kumuhana so people can see how to do things differently. We can figure this thing out. Capitalism is not where the moʻo lives. That is more interesting to me and it takes more of my life. I want to give light to that. We are in trouble, a lot of our people are homeless and that's not the issue. The whole society is an issue. One of my favorite quotes is by Krishnamurti, I listened to him talk in Santa Barbara in 1977 or '78, he must have been close to ninety at that time. He said, "It is no measure of health to be well adjusted to a profoundly sick society." This society was not accepting of me.

I had to find out that the problem wasn't me, it was society. No need get mad, just get clear. That helps me. I was fighting so hard to get Hawaiian in universities. Fucking universities, they're part of the problem. But, I am going to be a great professor for my students because this society is sick. I don't really want to fit in. Owning property, this and that, it's never been my thing. Even going to the doctor and all that kind of stuff. I'm in a different jag in this world.

I think my orientation has allowed me to have this time, to be kukamonga and to be thoughtful about these things in other ways. You gotta have people and it said in this aikane article, they lived in the outskirts of society. They did. We live, I live, and I have always been an outsider, always wondering why they never accepted me. Now I am thinking, "Yay!" This is the first discussion of this nature for me because I never felt compelled, so energetically it never came. I'm too interested in food sovereignty, radical transformation of our schooling systems.

When it couldn't be changed, I'm like okay, let's do our own. That is why I went to the Wānanga, they did their own. They did it themselves. I was learning with a bunch of radical thinkers, who didn't care what your orientation was. They just cared if you were a freedom fighter.

I was not always this way, orientation was not my issue. I am grateful that Kuʻumeaaloha stood up and others when I couldn't and I didn't, I wouldn't. Wasn't my issue. But she stood up and I was grateful. Being a homophobic, self-loathing, Hilo girl as I was. I was private in my hits, she was public and so thank you Kuʻumeaaloha, thank you.

I think, "ʻAʻohe pau ka ʻike i ka hālau hoʻokahi"[2] has been very helpful. It saved my life when all these others guys would try to put the kīhei on me on the wrong side, in front of 2,000 people, they try and do the kīhei like I didn't know shit right, I go, "Eh, ʻaʻohe pau ka ʻike i ka hālau hoʻokahi." You guys put your kīhei on the right side, I put it on my left side and here's why, shoot." If you don't know yourself you're going to be dragged around by the culture cops, by the you know, homophobic people. Like no, no, no. Not going to be dragged around anymore. Let me just love you instead. That was a decade ago. It takes a lot to love yourself, and when you get there, god you're grateful for surviving.

I give talks to the mental health association now, the suicide group. I thank them for the work they do and I tell them I am a gay woman and they all gasp, like a gay person cannot be their speaker. So, you got to love yourself, it has been my life's work. To love yourself, to love myself, and that's what Aotearoa taught me too. Geography shapes our knowing, that's part of the Hawaiian epistemology. Look around, go surf, go swim, go holoholo, go swim in the muliwai, go do something. Hawaiʻi is pretty special. I think it is going to be a key operating principle on the planet. I mean it, really, aloha. You see how it sheds through my insecurities, sheds, sheds past my other years, around my self-loathing. When you go into this frequency, you're in a different mode of behaving, thinking. People try to insult you, but brah, good luck. Their wives probably don't like them, poor thing. You begin to see the world differently, things become funny. Humorous, not funny. And kaumaha. Turn off the TV because there's so much hatred. Society is not smart, America is not teaching us anything. We are waking up together. These

---

2. This ʻōlelo noʻeau #203 or wise saying is translated as "All knowledge is not taught in the same school," which means that not all knowledge can be found in one place. Mary Kawena Pukuʻi (editor and translator), *ʻŌlelo Noʻeau: Hawaiian Proverbs & Poetical Sayings*, Bernice P. Bishop Museum Special Publication (Honolulu: Bishop Museum Press, 1983), https://search-ebsohost-com.eres.library.manoa.hawaii.edu/login.aspx?direct=true&db=nlebk&AN=2575808&site=ehost-live.

conversations help me understand that. I have new comrades in freedom. You go forward and forgive your family. I forgave my mom a long time ago, both are gone now. She forgave herself. Everyone needs to forgive each other, forgiveness is key.

I learned in Aotearoa that "mihi" means forgiveness. This big guy got up and said, "I'd like to mihi you" and I didn't know that mihi was a form of mentoring. He would speak of what he learned from what I said and it was just loving. So mihi is a way to summarize a person's ideas, it's an oracy tool, and so we brought it home to Hawai'i. We mihi each other at the end of classes, end of conferences, and people always say that's the highlight of the conferences. When people stand up and tell you what they learned and its impact on you. We're learning from each other. It's really an important oral practice, the mihi. I think Christianity turned it into forgiveness, but it's still love. Love mentors. Even from a stranger. It's found its grounding here in Hawai'i. It's being used in ho'oponopono too and I learned that there is no ho'oponopono before Christianity came. I was shocked to learn this. Ho'opono is, ho'oponopono is different in every setting. It's not one size fits all, it's diverse because it's all about aloha and pono. All of it.

8

Bradford Lum
Becoming a Mentor

Hawaiian renaissance and my own coming out was separate. School was separate, work was separate. I wasn't a whole person. I couldn't be a whole person. Everything was like, oh I gotta hide this, I gotta hide this 'cause I dance hula and I was worried my friends would think I'm māhū. I immersed myself in studies more than anything else. These parts of myself only came together when I left to San Francisco.

My name is Bradford Yin Jong Ikemanu Lum. I was born and raised in McCully, on Lime Street. I went to Lunalilo Elementary School, McKinley High School, and the University of Hawai'i. I graduated from UH in 1976 with a degree in Communications and Secondary Education. I came out as a gay man when I was eighteen years old. It was pretty amazing because I just made a decision for myself and said I was going to do it after high school. I was not going to do it in high school, but after. It was the best move for me because there was a group of māhū who dressed up in high school. I lived a double life. I remember and I feel really bad about it now because I used to tease them a lot. But, they are my friends now. I guess in a way I was teasing myself, it makes sense now, but that was where I was at.

In 1971 everything was hush hush. When you came out you had no role models, I only had straight friends. I told my best straight friend my freshman year at University of Hawai'i. He freaked out! I reminded him that we were very close and shared the most intimate parts of our lives and I never did anything. I asked him, "Did I ever make a pass at you?" He goes, "No." So what's the problem then?

I was really lonely and I hate to say that being an eighteen-year-old man or boy, coming out, there was literally no mentor at all. I found myself wanting attraction and I heard through the grapevine where men would hang out. So I went to Kapi'olani Park and I would go to this other place on campus where all the guys were playing around in the bathroom. I would go and I knew these weren't the greatest places for me to find any mentors. Until I was nineteen, a sophomore at UH and then I met this beautiful blond, blue-eyed guy who was thirty-five years old and gorgeous and I fell in love with him. He was a successful man, businessman in San Diego and I fell in love with the guy and he fell in love with me. We

Bradford Lum. Courtesy of Bradford Lum.

had this really long relationship. It was sexual, it wasn't you know, solid. My parents met him and everything, he came to my graduation. When I graduated from UH, my parents kept on asking, "Where's Jim?" I used to go to San Diego a lot to visit him. He used to come to visit me as well, so it was a hot and heavy relationship. Later on, Jim and I became friends. I started to grow up and I got too old for him. I realized that Jim liked playing with younger guys, I told him he had to stop it. We were super close.

I was always in relationships, I didn't like playing around. I found it cheap. I wished I had mentors. When I was eighteen at UH as a freshman, the drinking age was eighteen, so I went to Hulas. That's where I went and it was like boom! But, it wasn't Hulas yet, it was called the Gay 90s. It was where the Landmark Condominiums is. Right at that stoplight, used to be the entrance and when the traffic was red, it would stop right there and the boys would stand against the wall. Charley's Taxi used to be there. The boys would stand against the wall and wait for the traffic light to turn green and then a whole bunch of boys would go rushing into the bar. That is how paranoid it was.

I told my parents I was gay and it was pretty rough. My mom always knew, but my dad never accepted me. My dad had this idea that gay boys are feminine, but I loved sports so it did not make sense to him. Sports and music was the only way that I could communicate with my dad. I come from a musical family, my mom played with all the māhūs and everything. It was really hard for me when I would go into the bars because my mom's friends would all see me at the bars. "Oh, guess what? I saw your son at the bar and he was kissing somebody!" My mom had to put her foot down and she said, "The next time somebody comes to me and says something about you kissing any boy in the bar, you better quit it!"

I graduated in 1976 and wanted to become a hula dancer, but my father just couldn't understand. He would say, "I cannot understand why you like dance with all those māhūs." It's like hello, you want to see us dance hula? Back then it was really tough. Men did not really dance anymore. There were men hālau, but it was new to see a male hula dancer. It was so new. My parents were very religious as well. I was super confused. I immersed myself in work and school. I was the front desk office manager for Colony Resorts, where I worked while going to school too. I worked my ass off. Right after graduating I became assistant manager, which was an honor.

Protest & UH

When I was a senior at UH there was no Hawaiian Studies program, no Hawaiian Studies college period. We fought for it. We actually slept at Bachman and I got reminded of it when Mauna Kea happened. I was so happy to be with the young people at Bachman Hall and to be an alumni sitting with them. In my days it was really different. We were in the hallway, they couldn't even move. Those days were very important. When I was a freshman at UH, there was only an Ethnic Studies class, one Hawaiian Studies, that's it. There was nothing, zilch. I remember Puanani Burgess was my mentor and professor and I loved her to death because she was the one that really carried me over to my Hawaiian side. She was the one, not my parents, not my mother, even though she was playing Hawaiian music, I didn't like Hawaiian music at all. She was the one. It took someone outside my family to have me realize how important my Hawaiianness is. She said, "How many of you speak the language? How many of you are Native Hawaiian in this classroom?" There was about fifty of us. Then she said, "How many of you speak the language? Nobody! How many of you do hula? How many of you do this? Do that?" and then maybe two people raised their hands. She started to cry. Those tears were very sincere and she said, "Our people are dying. You people are the lucky ones. The Native Hawaiians that can come up to this University, you made it." And it was a big deal. To have Native Hawaiians come to the University of Hawaiʻi, it was a big deal and it changed my mindset. I didn't consider myself Native Hawaiian, I thought of myself as Chinese and it was safer to think that than saying I was Native Hawaiian. That was the really hard part. I remember in high school my friends would meet my mom and then look at me and ask, "What happened to you?" 'Cause she was really pretty, she was hapa, Hawaiian-haole.

Puanani Burgess got me to dance hula with/under Kahaʻi Topolinski. Kahaʻi was one of the men, besides Robert Cazimero that were up and coming kumu hula that graduated from Aunty Maiki. They committed to having men dance. I was telling my parents and my fada goes, "Oh since when you dance hula?" I was pretty serious and my sophomore year we started kanikapila at the University of Hawaiʻi. I have a smile on my face because those were the days. For the first time in Hawaiian history to have all like Gabby Pahinui, Aunty Genoa Keawe, all those entertainers, like Hui ʻOhana, Olomana, all on one stage. And all the hālau, it was so big and sold out. I was helping with the organizing and my mom was trying to get tickets. It was sold-out two nights. The kanikapila became the catalyst for the Hawaiian Studies program. If it wasn't for kanikapila I don't think that's when the renaissance started to happen. It was huge. For me, even in the Hawaiian part was unsure, Puanani kept pushing me and a whole bunch of us, telling us we going to be leaders one day. I used to laugh in her face, I never saw myself that way.

But Hawaiian renaissance and my own coming out was separate. School was separate, work was separate. I wasn't a whole person. I couldn't be a whole person. Everything was like, oh I gotta hide this, I gotta hide this 'cause I dance hula and I was worried my friends would think I'm māhū. I immersed myself in studies more than anything else. These parts of myself only came together when I left to San Francisco. That's when it all meshed.

In 1982 I had had it, I felt so done, so I left Honolulu. I left Hawaiʻi for the first time and my father freaked. He was worried because I did not have a job. He was the type of man that worked, you kept a job, you do all those things, you get married. That's my father's idea. My mom was more, as long as you're happy. Mom was cool. Dad was really hard on me. He was so pissed off. I had saved up, I left with twenty grand and back in 1982 that was really a lot of money.

Back in those days you could go see people off right at the gate with leis and everything. People singing to you, that kind of stuff. There was a whole bunch of people and I remember seeing my father and mother talk, and he goes to my mom, "I going bet you 100 dollahs the kid never coming back" and I always was the kid, never a grown-up man. Always the kid. My mom said, "I bet you he come back in a year." He said, "The kid never going come back, neither for you or for me, he's gone!" My mom said, "'Cause of you, 'cause you can't accept your son for being gay."

San Francisco

So I left for San Francisco. My first job was working at the Pearl Factory at Pier 39, digging out pearls. My father freaked again! He was swearing on the phone, asking how much money I make. I made about a thousand dollars a week and my father could not believe it. He was swearing at me on the phone, I had to send him my pay stubs so he would believe me. Good thing we did not have texts back then, I actually sent it to him.

I created my own family in San Francisco and I grew up a lot there. I met the dream of my life in San Francisco, we were together for six years. Anyway, I met this wonderful man I was with for six years. I started working at the Four Seasons. I did not want to work at a hotel because I wanted holidays off, but in the interview, the money was so good and I had the holidays and weekends off too. I became the payroll manager for like nine years.

I had to go to San Francisco to become the person I was going to be. When I was there it was at the height of the AIDS epidemic. I joined ACTUP and I felt strong for the first time in my whole life. My first gay pride parade I cried like a baby because there was so many people. It was the first time I felt powerful. I created my own family, my own home, my partner and I. I had met his parents, they were so wonderful, they would come over all the time. It started to feel like it was time for him to meet mine. I started stressing out when my parents were coming.

I went to pick them up at the airport and my father was shocked to see me driving. Like, "Whose car is this? How much you went pay?" and my mom had to tell him to cut it out because I was successful. He questioned everything, asking how much stuff costs. He comes to my apartment, asks how I can afford my nice furniture. He was impressed with the floors. My boyfriend at the time was an artist, so he painted. He did the floors, walls, kitchen, everything, it was beautiful. My dad was typical local asking who does all this stuff. The next morning I was making breakfast for everybody and my dad goes, "Who taught you how to cook?"

I remember I went into Kent and I's room and told him I had it with my father! Kent said I needed to tell my dad to lay off, so I got dressed in my suit and my father is already asking if I dress like that every day. I had to explain to him that I wear a different suit, this is white collah, not blue collah. I told him right then, "If you don't like the way I live, there is the door, I can buy you the first plane out of here right now." My mom wanted to stay and go shopping. He got quiet after that. The next day we had a huge dinner to honor my parents. It was rough. My dad did not talk, my mom was talking with everybody, drag queens everything. She thought all my friends were so nice, but my dad just went into the room to sleep. I felt really uncomfortable.

I joined ACTUP to help with AIDS funding because there was nothing. If you look at the *Bay Area Reporter*, which was a weekly newspaper, there were pages and pages of men dying. It came to one point when I was looking for my friends. I had many friends die from HIV and AIDS. It hit home for me. I wanted to do something. I could not just go to work, make money, have fun, go to dinner with my boyfriend. I needed to do something. Both of us were members of ACTUP. In 1984 or 1986 the Democratic National Convention was in San Francisco and ACTUP was a big part of that. We stopped traffic in San Francisco for six hours. There were riot police all around us. We were holding hands, I remember Kent turning to me and saying he hoped we weren't separated if they put us in the can. But I knew the organizers had money and could bail us out. The riot police actually did not do anything to us. Right then and there because of our action, the San Francisco legislature, our board of supervisors, knew they had to do something about this. San Francisco was the first city in the country to help people with AIDS and HIV. The very first.

In 1986 there was the first AIDS International Doctors conference. I will never forget it. Nordstrom at that time fired four people with AIDS. They fired them because they did not want to pay for their medical expenses. We responded with a huge march down Market Street. Nobody knew we were going to do it. ACTUP would wear these black shirts. I was so angry. Part of that anger came from my childhood, from my family, it was my way of expressing who I really was with my brothers and sisters. It was a way to make sure that funding went to everything. I felt very powerful.

I was also a member of the Gay Men's Business Association. We used to have mixers every Friday and it was kind of bougie. All white-collar men in their suits, having a cocktail, networking with each other. It was really cool. I also belonged to the GAPA, Gay Asian Pacific Alliance. I remember one year they came to me and they go, "Eh Brad, can you make haku leis for like 200?" I was like, are you nuts?! I got some ferns and braided the damn thing. They helped me braid. For some reason this local boy, was like, "That's not how we do it in Hawai'i." I had to put him in his place. I looked at him and said, "Oh dude, you are barking up the wrong tree!" I was just becoming a kumu hula at that time for Aunty Linda David. She puka-ed me in 1990. It was hard to tell a young person off. I was so angry, very angry, but we got through that. I was still a member of GAPA. In 1995 we had a huge Hawai'i contingent in the Chinatown of San Francisco. Was our hālau and Patrick Makuakāne's halau. Was me and him and we did it like, they did their motions and we did ours, and the girls did the pū'ili, and just whatever, one line Patrick, one line mine and it just worked! It looked great. We had 200 hula dancers. It was pretty amazing.

The best thing I did was leave for San Francisco and have my own family. I really encourage anyone to leave. You can always come back. I came back. Once you come back, you seen the world. You seen how it is. I had to fight for my position. Many times in San Francisco I had to fight to be who I was, people wanted to change me. You can't change me. That made a huge difference in my life. I think the biggest part was ACTUP and how militant I got. I got so militant, it wasn't even funny man. My mom was so paranoid. She was freaking out because she saw on the news about ACTUP and people getting arrested. I told her not to worry because I was going to do what I wanted to do. My parents were always trying to control me because I was the baby of the family. I think ACTUP in Hawai'i was very conservative and I wasn't. I wanted to fight. It wasn't so much about fighting for ACTUP, it was about really fighting for my life, fighting for my rights, fighting for everything that was taken from me and also hidden, or trying to hide who I was. I was like, you cannot do that to me! That was a big thing. Huge.

San Francisco was a really big success for me. In 1995 my father called, tells me my mom has cancer and that he has diabetes, high blood pressure, and an aneurysm in his brain. He asks me to come home. At first, I was like no. I was making 45K at Four Seasons, which was good money in those days. My life was so good, I went to the best concerts, I saw Bette Midler, everything, all the plays for free. I grumbled at him and he hung up. I was so frustrated, but finally, I said yes, and even though I did not want to, I came home.

Returning Home

I have two older brothers, but they're lazy. My father picked me because I am the smart one, the first one graduate from college, the one who went to San Francisco. My mom told me my dad would brag about me, the son that worked for the Four Seasons with the fancy office. I broke down and came home. My partner would not come with me to Hawai'i because he felt my parents hated him. Which was true. At first I was in denial, I asked him to come. We had to break up. That was my last solid relationship, since 1995. We were both brokenhearted on different levels. I come back home to take care my parents. My father then tells me I cannot "play with boys" and I was like, "WHAT?!" I came home to take care of them, "Don't tell me what to do with my life, if I want to play with boys, I'll play with the boys." So you know, since then I had a lot of superficial relationships and one of them I thought was going to be really good, but unfortunately not. He was also a kumu hula and went to jail, but I am not going to say his name. He went to jail, it broke my heart because he was on meth. I can't do that. Just before he got arrested he came to my door and begged me to let him in, but no, I cannot help you if you are on that thing, you have to get clean first.

So, my father's health was deteriorating. He was a big musician back in the '30s and '40s. He used to have a band called Charlie Lum and the Hatchet Men, a 36-piece orchestra that he conducted. He was a real talent. You could give him a tone and he would write it on paper. He was so talented. Robert Cazimero used to come to my father just for that. My father was really akamai when it came to sound. That's how really good he was. Anyway, one day after dialysis we had to go to the Musicians union because they were doing a picture book of those days. He was looking at all the pictures, sitting in the car, I will never forget it. He started talking about the good old days and then all of a sudden the man started to bawl. Like a heaving bawl with snot coming out of his nose and he could hardly talk. I asked if he was okay and he wipes the tears away and said, "I have never seen a nicer man like you. You came home, from your cushy job in San Francisco, to come and take care of me and I don't see you play with any boys, but that's your life. I don't want to stop you from doing that." I was like, huh? Is this the Charlie Lum that I know? He laughed at me, he somehow needed to tell me that. He kept going on that I'm the kindest, beautiful man. Then he tells me, "I used to have a relationship with a guy too." I could not believe it, "No way! What happened?" He said, "No, I never like, Chinese, conservative, should have never happened, it never transpired." When I asked more, he explained that he was too young back in those days. I remember taking him home that day, his eyes was all bloodshot from crying, he walked straight into the room. My mom was like, "What happened?" and I said, "I think Dad's going to die" and four months later my dad had five strokes in two hours.

Having my dad say that to me was an accomplishment. I never thought I would hear it from him, never thought I would see it. Just before my father passed away a friend of mine asked if I had gotten my teaching degree and suggested that I teach elementary school. At that time, I had my mom to take care of too. It is really hard to be a caregiver. Super hard. Super hard when you have two brothers who don't accept your lifestyle. My father passed away at ninety-six.

I owned an apartment taking care of Mom. My mom wanted to buy a house and I thought we should do it, that's what she wanted, it was her money. I am a doer, I am not all talk. So we did it. Took Mom and got the house. I will never forget that on November 30th he passed away. His memorial service was December 4th. That was hard and nobody in the family wanted to do anything. I had to do everything. I had to do all the funeral arrangements. No one knew how they wanted to dress Dad. So I had to do it. I said, "Don't complain when you see his suit on." He had a favorite suit, a very loud, Filipino green suit. So no one complained. My mom thought the service was nice, but I had to do everything. It was hell. Hellish. My mom wanted to get the house, we do it, we go to football games, volleyball games. Finally one day we are going to the volleyball game and I was working as a teacher and Mom came with me every day to school because I wanted to make sure she was okay. I worked at Kalihi Kai and then Kalihi Uka, Likelike. I was at Likelike when my mom passed away. Anyway, I was working and doing well. We go to a volleyball game and I asked my mom for her blessing. She laid into me and started swearing and I did not know where it came from. She got upset, saying I made her feel uncomfortable. We went home and everything was fine. We talked, agreed that I would see her after school. Later that day, I come home from work and my mom is gone, I called the police, called my brothers and my mom was with them, they accused me of hitting my mom. I could not believe it! I explained to them what happened, they did not believe me and they kicked me out of the house. I only had ten minutes to leave. I was homeless. I was a member of Unity Church at that time and Reverend Skye would not let me be homeless, they let me stay in the church for about four months. I eventually found a place all by myself. I had no connection to my family at all since then, nothing. That was 2005. For like four years I never saw my whole family. I hadn't heard from my brothers, my mother. All of a sudden, I get a call from a friend who says they just saw my mom's obituary. I said, "No, my mom never die. How you guys know that?" And they told me they saw the obituary that my mom passed away. I went nuts.

Seriously, I went cuckoo after that. I turned to drugs to escape, but I was smart enough to know the signs, I saved myself and put myself in the hospital. I needed help. I finally saw a psychiatrist who I still have a relationship with. I used to have to see her every day, then once a week and now it's like once a month just to check in. It took a long time to come to a place of peace for myself as a gay man. I retired in 2018 and I have to tell you even though I was distraught about my mom passing away, I felt a sigh of relief. I didn't need to fake it anymore. I could go to the gay bar and be who I am. The position I am in right now, it took me a long time to get out of that. In 2014 I was diagnosed with prostate cancer, bone cancer. Another trial and tribulation I had to get myself through. I had to pull myself together, cancer really helped me. Now I enjoy every day. There were times I was suicidal, thinking I was a bad person because of what happened with my parents. Now I know that my parents were codependent and it screwed me up in the head. It took me a while to meet some wonderful people in the community who have started to look at me as a mentor. I hope my story is teachable, that it shows anyone can overcome challenges. I had many experiences, I lived it, but I don't live in that house. My brother is still pissed off at me. I took him to court. I found out and this is what karma is, he sold the family plot for 2.5 million dollars. They caught my brother because the trust was in my name. I do not know what is going to happen. We just went to court, so we will see. He is in trouble because he was not supposed to sell the house if it's in my name. My friends are saying I can finally get revenge, but I do not want that, I am happy where I am at.

 I haven't been this happy in a very long time. I am happy with myself and I have a relationship with myself. I don't need a relationship with anybody. I don't need it. I'm happy just being with my friends and going out with them, we do so much together. I really like it, it seems like my life is back to where it was in San Francisco.

 When I left Hawaiʻi, it was very conservative. Hawaiʻi was not ready for gay pride. We used to have gay pride parades in Honolulu and it was like fifteen minutes long, so I never went. But from then, it grew. It's an honor to be a mentor and I really believe that I am. I am a Buddhist now. I use my teachings when I'm giving people suggestions. I don't take any BS either. The other day I got angry and my friends never seen me like this. We were sitting right in from Kaimana Beach. There were a whole of bunch of people with chairs, I assumed they were staying at the Kaimana because they kept going in and out and all of a sudden this guy opened his big mouth and was like "6 feet, you're too close to me!" and I was like, "Hello, you don't own the beach! If you are that paranoid about people sitting close to you, then go up to your condominium you poʻe haole." I was so angry! And he goes, "You swore at me!" I said, "Look it up, poʻe haole is white man" and my friends were like "Bravo!" I don't want to take any crap anymore from anybody, including my brother or my whole family. My therapist said I have come a long way.

Marriage Equality

When I came back to Hawaiʻi, I was one of the first people to get involved in the marriage initiative. In 1990 that is when it started. I came home and got involved. Dave Foley, Dr. McEwan, they all became my friends. I was the chanter a lot, they used me as that person. I think in 1999, I was head of a candlelight vigil. I was also part of the Prince Kūhiō Civic club so I got them to sing. It was a huge thing. I got Aunty Vicky Holt Takamine to talk, some other major Hawaiians to talk as well. That was a huge deal. I also belonging to equality Hawaiʻi, I was on the board for a short time. There was lots of infighting, I did not like it. They fought a lot about leadership. I got so sick of spending hours and hours of people fighting. I told them, I would be on the side because they weren't even focusing on the policies. I still played a major role in the whole marriage thing. I remember the filibuster days. I will never forget that day. I was inside and they kept going on and on. I heard the other side and our side and then we heard the māhūs were yelling and screaming. I came outside and I remember them saying, call your friends, call everybody right now! And I am not joking, there were more than 5,000 of us and our allies together that day and night. It was all day. We had testimony too, I was sixth. At the time I had started a foundation called Hulumanu Foundation. I got the name Hulumanu because he was King Kamehameha IV's aikāne, which had different names, one of them was Hulumanu. I liked that name so much and our goal was to give a voice to Hawaiian teenagers, if they got kicked out, if they needed a home. We helped them get placed, food, giving them opportunities. It worked out really well that time, it made me really happy. I testified early, there were like 3,000 people. I testified about aikāne. I talked about how the change in religion destroyed Hawaiian culture. I told them how angry I was, that they forgot our Hawaiian systems, how we were free, how it was easy, that if you loved someone, it didn't matter. Until, the missionaries came and changed everything. People forget that. I said, "So you're telling me that you remember what your kūpuna did, but you sure you can't remember about that?" They erased us from their poʻo. I was so angry that night. Before I even testified, I remember staying by the door with a small group of us. All of a sudden there was this big group of Jesus Christ people singing and I am not joking, it was the first time I felt intimidated. I was right by the door and these big Samoan guys pushed their way in and said, "Jesus Christ won! You lost." I started to cry, I could not stop. I thought Hawaiʻi was a good place to love. I thought Hawaiʻi was a place of acceptance and being tolerant rather than being intolerant. I had never seen so much bigotry in my life.

Then people saw me crying and all these people tried to help. The security guards came and got the big guys out of there because they were bullying us when we were just standing there. Everyone was so thankful that I spoke up and got them out of there. That is the kind of person I am. In 2013 when marriage started to happen, I decided to become a minister myself so I could marry people as well. The first same-sex wedding I did, I could not stop crying. It was an emotional rollercoaster.

I remember Kai Kahele's father gave a speech, I wish I had a recording, he was so eloquent and beautiful, almost the same as my speech. His speech said that we cannot turn our backs on people when they simply love each other. That's how it was in old Hawai'i. I cried when I heard his testimony. So Kai Kahele, Chris Lee, Kaniela Ing all became my best friends because of that. Mina Morita from Kaua'i asked me to pule at the capital and it was such an honor!

As far as politics go, people would tell me I would be good, but I felt like it was too dirty, too pilau for me. My 'ano is not ready for that. I cannot be like that. That was one of the hardest fights we ever did. When it did pass we were so happy. The Senate passed it, Abercrombie was ready to sign it, I was there at the signing. It was so awesome, a really great time. Finally!

I think the older I get though, I am tired. I just want to do what I am doing now. I love my friends, my gay friends are my family. I love them to pieces. I also play kickball, I am in the Hawai'i kickball league. We only won three games, but at the end of the season I was voted unanimously as most caring. It just shows you where I am at today. It's great because I get asked to start the 'oli, although this year in the pandemic, we did not do the parade. But, there is always next year. The pandemic is not fun, I tell you on the mainland, people don't care, they don't wear their masks. I got really concerned about going in the gay clubs, it's bad. Luckily I have not gotten COVID. I really think that ke akua has taken care of me because I take care of myself. That is the biggest thing right now, I am getting tired of the pandemic. I am so tired. I have done a lot and some things are on the back burner. Even though I have the title of a Kumu Hula, it's not where I am right now. I just want to be gay and happy. I think that's my first priority, because the older I get, who knows what is going to happen to me tomorrow? I don't know if I am going to be around, but I think doing this gives me an idea of where I am at. I want to be happy. I want to enjoy life. I want to travel. I want to mentor people. I have started to already. I am lucky that way. I am blessed that I can do that.

Lani Ka'ahumanu
Assimilation = Spiritual Erasure

In the next few months, I will be seventy-nine and cruising into my 80s. Unbelievable how time passes and lives change. My son is fifty-seven and my daughter, fifty-five. She identifies as bisexual and her daughter, my granddaughter Molly, just turned fifteen. She belongs to the Gay-Straight Alliance at her high school. In early June, she texted that she wanted to march in the San Francisco LGBT Pride Parade and asked if I would take her. I was thrilled! I love marching in the Pride Parade. I had marched in the Pride Parade for over 20 years. First as a lesbian, and then as a bisexual. What's not to love? People cheering you for being yourself! The last time I'd marched with the Bay Area Bisexual Network [BABN] contingent. This time, Molly and I marched with the expanded Bay Area Bi+ & Pan Network [BABPN]. On parade day the energy was high. A million people attend San Francisco Pride. We located our contingent and waited for our turn to join the parade. I introduced Molly to the folks I knew, and she came out to me as pan. Someone gave her a pan flag that quickly became a cape for the two-mile walk down Market Street. It was awesome.

I live on the California coast, fourteen miles north of the Russian River flowing into the Pacific. My little house is two miles up from the ocean. I love it here. It's a two-and-a-half-hour drive to San Francisco. I moved away from the city to write my activist memoir, "My Grassroots Are Showing." But my life has taken unexpected turns, including becoming my son's caregiver. Having dedicated time for focused writing has been limited and I continue to write. Living rurally has been a blessing in so many ways, especially during the COVID lockdown.

In my 45-plus years of LGBTQ activism and organizing on the continent I've met only a few Kānaka Maoli. I always identified with the API community but I'm realizing I have never experienced a Kanaka Maoli Lesbian Gay Bi+ Māhū community holding me in my day-to-day life. Saying this gives me a lump in my throat. I was thirty-six years old before I stepped foot on Hawaiian lepo/soil and began my aloha 'āina journey. Being Kanaka Maoli is a source of joy planted deep inside my being. My struggle has been passing for haole and somehow feeling I wasn't *enough because of my light skin. Like I'm a faux Kanaka Maoli or something. Sounds ridiculous when I say that, but there it is. My Kanaka Maoli experience, my moʻolelo comes through my mother's moʻolelo and the pride she gifted me from the moment I was conceived.*

I was born in Edmonton, Alberta, Canada, on October 5, 1943, to John and Minerva Helani Farrell. My parents met on Waikīkī during World War II, where they fell in love, married, and pretty quickly were expecting me. My dad was a civil engineer and a Marine who received orders to go to Canada to help build the AlCan (Alaska/Canada) Highway and airplane runways in the Aleutian Islands.

Leprechauns and Menehunes

My dad's family moved from Duluth, Minnesota, to San Francisco in the early 1940s. His mother, my grandma Pat Farrell, was my only living grandparent. There was much talk of being Irish from County Cork. I grew up with stories of leprechauns and menehunes. Grandma Pat spoke a little Yiddish because, as the story went, "she worked with Jewish families who'd just had a baby" or something. My cousin who delved into this side of family history told me our Grandma Pat's given name was Hattie Rathke. She spoke fluent Polish and Yiddish. My hidden Jewish roots post-WWII.

My Mama's Moʻolelo

My mom was born in Yokohama in 1920 and raised in Kobe on a private compound with her older brother Jim, parents, great-grandmother, and servants. There were koi ponds, tennis courts, and manicured gardens. She had a personal servant. Her brother had two servants because he was a boy. They wore hand-sewn clothing and went to a private school. My grandmother Annie Helanikulani managed the home. Their great-grandmother refused English, Christianity, and Western clothes. She spoke Japanese, wore kimono, had a Shinto shrine, tatami, and futon. Both children spoke and wrote Japanese. Her parents had a successful import/export business and socialized with the Embassy crowd. They were Hawaiian, Japanese, Euro-colonial settler mix. The mix didn't sit well with their social class.

When my mom was ten, her mother, my grandmother, fell seriously ill. Doctors came and went for more than a month. The children were given no information and were not allowed to be physically near her. Their father and doctors decided she and the children would sail to Hawaiʻi, where there would be more help. The children would stay with my grandmother's older sister, my Aunty Emma in Honolulu. My grandfather James would stay in Japan to take care of the business.

My mom didn't speak of her mother's leprosy, the Hansen's disease diagnosis, or details until I was an adult and only then was it in hushed tones. Her mother had been wearing large hats with a veil covering her face and gloves so she wouldn't frighten the children. The hat, veil, and gloves also hid her illness on the voyage. She was traveling illegally. My grandfather had business connections and coordinated the trip. When they arrived in Honolulu in 1931 my grandmother went to a sanitarium. My mom and her brother went to Aunty Emma's.

Waikīkī, Lalani Village—Early 1930s

Both my Aunty Emma and her husband Uncle George Mossman, a master ʻukulele builder, had been concerned by the growing Westernization of Hawaiʻi and the loss of Hawaiian culture and language. In 1932 they were committed to preserving and teaching ancient ways and created the Lalani Village next to their home on Waikīkī.

My mother and her brother Jim went from a close-knit privileged protected family life in Japan to join Aunty Emma and Uncle George's large family—barefoot, beach clothing, and working with the family at Lalani Village. A master hale craftsperson built traditional grass huts to provide a sense of ancient Hawaiian community. Well-known kumu hula, performers, and chanters came to live in the dwellings to demonstrate, teach, and perform.

This is where my mother lived and learned the hula. She loved dancing, excelled, and eventually danced and taught at Lalani Village. She described the hale, and the visitors, sailors, and local Kānaka Maoli. My mom's first love and focus were dancing and teaching the hula. She became an accomplished dancer. So much so, the *LA Times* did a photo essay on her in 1939. She told us stories of Waikīkī beach in the 1930s, stories of earning five cents and a bag lunch for being an extra in the Hollywood "jungle" movies being shot there, stories of surfing and Duke Kahanamoku and his brothers, and of the paniolo/Hawaiian cowboys. A tale we often heard was about a sailor who didn't know how to surf. His board hit my mother's shoulder, giving her chronic bursitis. We always heard that story when she was ironing our school uniforms. My grandmother Annie died in 1932 and my grandfather James died of TB in Japan in 1938.

My Moʻolelo

I met my Aunty Emma once when I was seven or eight years old. We'd moved from San Francisco and lived in the suburbs on the San Francisco Peninsula. She was Mormon leading a small tour to Salt Lake City. There was a layover at the San Francisco Airport not far from where we lived. When she walked into our home, I felt like I was in the presence of royalty, like she was a queen. She was warm with an easy smile, beautiful, stood tall, and sat very straight. I don't remember what was said but the image of her standing in the doorway and sitting in a red chair is still with me.

I am the oldest of four girls and the only child given a Hawaiian name. I felt a special sense of pride in my name—Lani. My mother told me her mother's name was Helanikulani, and she was Helani, and I was Lani. I never met anyone with my name growing up in the 1940s/'50s. In the late 1940s when my mom registered me for first grade at St. Bruno's school, Sister Theophane took my hand and told me "Lani is a heathen name. We will call you Marjorie," my other name. I didn't know what a heathen was, but it didn't sound very good. On the way home I asked my mom about it. She laughed. "They don't know anything." She always brushed things off with a laugh. I soon learned about heathens. Sister Theophane had a can on her desk with a photo of a Maryknoll missionary surrounded by smiling dark-skinned children. The priest was holding a pagan baby, a heathen who had been baptized and saved. We donated our two cents change left from our milk money to help this important work. I went to St. Bruno's for eight years. Whenever we studied Japan, I brought Nori seaweed to share and kimonos and for Hawaiʻi I talked about the hula and how the movements told a story and that my mom danced the hula. I also shared that King Kamehameha, who united the islands, was my great-great-great-great-great-uncle. I liked sharing about my family.

My sisters and my friends hung out at our home. My mom's warm aloha spirit welcomed everyone. We all loved listening to her stories. She loved telling them. She taught the hula to all of us kids in our two-car garage. She never stopped telling stories about Hawaiʻi but as the years passed there were fewer details. Having four children in seven years was overwhelming. I think she was also worn down by cultural insensitivity and ignorance, being humored and exoticized, and having in-laws who worried among themselves that each pregnancy might bring the shame of dark skin and flat nose. They'd breathed a sigh of relief when I was born light-skinned, round-eyed, with a button nose. My sister, two years younger, looked like my mom and had olive skin that tanned dark in the summer. She was called picaninny and little monkey. I was told I was lucky to have the golden skin. I was perplexed. I loved it when my mom called me a "kanaka."

The Sixties—Marriage, Motherhood, Feminism

I was raised to be a wife, and the mother of many children. When I was nineteen, I married my high school sweetheart, the captain of the football team. My mom danced to the "Hawaiian Wedding Song" for us at the reception. Within five years we had two children, and my husband was hired to teach at the high school where we met. I was twenty-four years old, a full-time suburban housewife and mother. It was the late sixties. We marched against the Vietnam War. I joined Another Mother for Peace, and spoke out against the war, inter-continental ballistic missiles (ICBMs), and nukes. I saw Black Panther Bobby Seale talking about their free breakfast program for poor kids. I collected food and brought it to their headquarters. I heard Caesar Chavez talk about the United Farm Workers union organizing and I joined the successful grape boycott. I always identified with the people. I began taking a night class every semester at the local community college. I loved learning and doing something by and for myself. I promised myself a trip to Hawai'i if I ever graduated.

The women's movement and feminism began making more sense to me. Much to my family's dismay, I traded in my Mrs. for Ms.—an edgy radical move—branding me a feminist. Sounds pretty silly now, doesn't it? My husband didn't care one way or the other. We were best friends, but we grew up to be different people. I'd done everything I was raised to be, but something wasn't right. I was crying all the time. Neither one of us knew why until one day he said he'd figured it out. "You need to leave," he said. "You've never had a life of your own. I'll keep the kids. You can't do what you need to do if they're with you." As soon as I heard this, I knew he was right. He loved me and let go. We did the best we knew how taking care of our children. Six weeks later I moved a couple miles away and instead of being a volunteer mom at my kids' school, I was hired as a teacher's aide. This was my first paid job.

Letting go of full-time mothering was, and still is, the most difficult thing I've ever done in my life. I cried my sadness out and knew in every cell of my being I had made the right decision. I trusted with all my heart things would work out for all of us. I never looked back once.

Lani Ka'ahumanu—Radicals, Lesbians, & Dykes

After my divorce I didn't want to go back to my maiden name, Lani Farrell. I told my mom I wanted people to know I was Hawaiian; I wanted a Hawaiian last name. Without hesitation she said "Ka'ahumanu is perfect for you. She was a radical in her day. She broke the food kapus and was a surfer." I had a difficult time pronouncing Kaʻahumanu at first. I practiced and tried it on and grew into my name—Lani Kaʻahumanu. Later I found out you're not supposed to take an aliʻi name unless they give it to you. Once though a few years later when I lived in Maui I went to Hana camping. By the time we arrived it was pitch-black. We weren't sure where to camp. We had no flashlight and just threw our sleeping bags on the grass next to the car. When we woke up, we found we were in a State Park a few yards from where Kaʻahumanu was born! I took this as an affirmative sign. I love my name and enjoy the mini educational opportunities when I assist people learning to say my name.

Life was brand new. I was in my early thirties and on my own for the first time in my life. I decided to transfer from the community college to San Francisco State University [SFSU] and moved to the City several months later. I met other feminists, lesbian feminists. These were out of the closet lesbians of all ages proudly reclaiming the term "Dyke," reclaiming their bodies, their vulvas, their vaginas, their menstrual blood, their clits, and orgasms. There were woman-identified-women-loving-women, and wiccans, and some were womyn, womon, wimmin, or wemoon. There were brilliant accessible professors everywhere all around me. I was swimming with the big kids and very excited, and very attracted, and a little nervous. I'd always had crushes on girls and women friends but never sexualized them. This was *very* different!

Back in the mid- to late '70s when you heard "women's" anything it pretty much equated to lesbian. Women's culture and music was exploding in the Bay Area. There were women-only concerts and dances, an all-women's auto repair business, and women's newspapers. Women's bookstores and cafes were popping up around the Bay. I became a student leader in the nascent Women Studies Department working with professors, adjuncts, and other students who taught me about heterosexism (what's now called heteronormativity), race and class privilege, and what it meant to be a woman in the patriarchy. Feminism gave me a language to understand my life experience and to trust myself. My personal was political.

Lesbians were challenging gay men on their sexism. The umbrella term gay did not include lesbians or lesbian issues such as having children and being involved in custody battles. Lesbians demanded to be recognized separately—as in a gay and lesbian community and movement! It took many years for this to take hold. Meanwhile lesbians were encouraging everyone, all of us to "Come Out!" Saying, "We're here for you!" Asking, "What are you waiting for?" I was swept away.

My lesbian coming-out process was thrilling, and awkward. My friend and I sat in her car outside our first "women"-only party. We were so anxious we couldn't get out of the car. After a couple hours of watching women go in or come out, we began laughing because the party was going to end before we made it inside.

We finally walked in and to my shock someone shouted, "Lani!" and it was the younger sister of someone I knew in high school. There I was at a lesbian party, and I knew the woman giving the party!

Coming out to my family, though, was very different. In their eyes I'd already committed the biggest sin of all—leaving my children, that's worse than leaving the Catholic church which I'd done in the sixties. So, coming out lesbian on top of leaving my children and everything else added another notch to my "outlaw" status.

My heart was finally home. I'd landed. I loved women. I was attracted to soft butch women but whenever a flirtatious attraction came along, I didn't stop myself from flirting back. I joined the Women Studies Hiring Committee and supported myself working at the Pregnancy Consultation Center answering phones, doing pregnancy tests, birth control and abortion counseling. I began to speak out as a lesbian mother. In the 1976 Gay Freedom Day March I marched arm in arm in the lesbian mother's contingent down Market Street shouting "2-4-6-8 are you sure your mother's straight?" It was glorious.

Graduation, March on Washington, Lesbian Chef, Lahaina

I graduated from Women Studies in 1979. I was the first in my family to graduate from college. My housewife dream of going to Hawai'i 11 years earlier had come true. I was burned out on school, activism, and completely exhausted. I needed a job to save for the trip. It's funny how it turned out. Cooking was one of the skills I picked up and refined as a housewife. My daughter says, "Remember the Village OZ camp I went to last summer? They need a chef." It was owned by millionaire hippies who left the city to raise their children on the land. I contacted them, cooked them dinner, and was interviewed. We hit it off. The owner, Redwood, told me, "It'd be great to have a lesbian chef."

OZ was a New Age, vegetarian, clothing-optional, back-to-the-land getaway in Northern California. There were cabins, a yurt, an old barn with a basketball court and library and bunk beds in the loft for people passing through. The place had a resident masseuse, a gardener, a handy guy, and me, the chef/community house manager.

I arrived a week after graduation. I put up my feminist posters in the kitchen. As the community house manager, I welcomed the guests and gave the what's-what intro talk. I was out, open, and comfortable, and loved being the lesbian chef.

A few weeks into the summer season Merry arrived. We fell madly in love. This was a major mutual head-over-heels in love relationship. I'd had girlfriends before, but this was head to toe, no hesitation electric. We were ecstatic. The shared attraction had never happened quite like that before. She joined the summer crew. We are still friends.

At the end of the summer season, before flying to Lahaina, I traveled to DC to attend the 1979 March on Washington for Lesbian and Gay Rights (MOW). This first national march was partially inspired by the assassination of gay icon Harvey Milk. There were 100,000 people there. Among other issues speakers demanded the end of discrimination in the federal government based on sexual orientation like in the military, government jobs, and federally contracted private employment. The march helped establish a national gay movement.

Two days after I arrived home from the MOW, I flew to Maui to live for six months and then I'd return to OZ for the summer season. I stayed with a friend's younger brother until I found a place. He lived on the ocean side of Front Street a few blocks down the road from Longhi's and other tourist and local restaurants. One of his housemates told me about a job opening. I was hired as a prep cook at the popular Aloha Cantina across from the Banyan Tree. On my first day the brunch/lunch cook cut her hand so badly she ended up in emergency getting stitches. I quickly became the back-up cook and ongoing prep cook.

I found a place to live on Front Street two miles from work. It took a little while to gather what I needed and get settled. I wrote to my mom about my life. I loved walking in the old Lahaina neighborhoods and talking with people. I bought a bicycle for my commute and began to explore. When I finally made it to the beach I dozed off in the warm sun and suddenly I was in a WWII movie. I heard planes and what I thought were bombs exploding. What the hell! I talked with local folks and found out Kahoʻolawe was a U.S. Navy bombing range. The bombing was so disturbing on so many levels to me I stopped going to the beach. I kept pursuing information and was heartened to hear about the ongoing activism. Everyone I spoke with told stories of activist George Helm and the others who had lost their lives two years earlier.

OZ and Coming Out Again

By the time I returned to OZ I was energized and ready to work. The large organic veggie garden was in the ground and spring flowers were in full bloom welcoming me. My kitchen posters had survived the winter. It was good to see everyone. A month into the season Bill Mack arrived intending to stay a couple days before heading up the coast. Everyone including guests had to do garden and kitchen karma yoga every day. I'd give them tasks to assist me with feeding our base of 15 and up to 100 people. The first time Bill arrived for karma yoga with me he noticed my posters and asked if I'd read Adrienne Rich's *Of Woman Born*.[1] I was curious a man wanted to talk about the institution of motherhood. Sure, I wanted to talk! We began to have these incredible discussions. My mind was a little blown. I didn't quite grasp what was happening. After a few days I realized we were flirting, and it went on from there.

He identified as a bisexual, and an anti-sexist activist and community organizer and saw feminism as a global philosophy and healing for the world. I was completely taken by surprise. We fell in love talking about organizing a feminist revolution, this was 1980! We talked about community organizing and movement building and women and men working together and feminist bisexuals being an inclusive unifying force. We even talked about doing a book of bisexual coming-out stories.

The only problem was I couldn't say I was bisexual. I had believed there was no such thing. I was so biphobic it was unthinkable. And yet there was no getting around the profound philosophical, spiritual, political, psychic, and sexual connection we had. We also shared the same sense of humor and laughed a lot. I think that saved me.

Coming Out Bisexual in San Francisco

Moving back to my San Francisco lesbian community was not an easy transition. Even if it felt sometimes scary and risky coming out as a lesbian it made sense—if you love and are attracted to women, you're a lesbian not heterosexual. Coming out as a bisexual was much more complex and challenging. I'd been a biphobic lesbian, so I knew what was coming my way. Bisexuals were traitors, untrustworthy, oversexed, male identified, and wishy-washy. Everything I'd ever heard about bisexuals was up in my face and I'd never heard anything positive. I was on the fence and needed to choose. There was NO middle ground. There was no visible community, no movement, no coming-out books, nothing to support my lesbian-coming-out-bisexual process. There were a couple books and a bit of research on married bisexual men but nothing for a lesbian falling in love with a man.

I had heard about a Bisexual Center (1976–1984) and decided to attend their women's coming-out group. Like me the women were in different stages of coming out bisexual. However, the group's coming-out focus was from a heterosexual experience and culture. I was grappling with a man in my life. My support would have to be found within my lesbian community. I saw what happened when a

---

1. Adrienne Cecile Rich, *Of Woman Born: Motherhood as Experience and Institution* (New York: W. W. Norton & Company, 1976).

lesbian fell for a man, they were no longer welcome in the community and so left to start a new life. I'd already left that life. I intended to stay. I knew I'd quickly find out who my friends were. Word spread fast, "Lani went back to men." Some reactions were irrational and shocking. Others were just plain cruel and included public shaming and shunning. My mom couldn't get her head around bisexual. She kept thinking Bill was a gay friend. My kids were teenagers by then and pretty blasé about the whole thing. My ex-husband "knew."

I found lesbian friends who could care less if I was a bisexual. I remained visible and active in the lesbian community, serving on committees, producing women's dances and events. I attended Asian Pacific Sisters events and gatherings for lesbian and bisexual women. I made several lasting friendships. The Lavender Godzilla men of the Gay Asian Pacific Alliance (GAPA) were fabulous supportive allies. (Lavender Godzilla was the name of their newsletter.)

The longer I was out the more lesbians and gay men came out to me in private. My phone number was passed around. People would call and say, "You don't know me but . . ." I became the confessional for many, including leaders who'd say, "Well actually I'm bisexual but I can't come out, I'd lose credibility," and then ask for advice. "You're braver than me, I can't be out." I knew I wasn't alone but the community I needed and wanted to organize was in a deep dark closet.

Because I was so out, my bisexual identity was challenged. I was on the hot seat. I learned how to handle challenges and educate. I spoke from my experience and talked about my own coming-out process and my internalized biphobia and misinformation. Doing it that way I could handle the heat. People thanked me and sometimes asked if they could talk with me. My answer was always YES. I loved talking with people. It relieved my isolation and was the nitty-gritty work of early bisexual community organizing and securing allies.

The Rise of HIV/AIDS

When I returned to the City in 1980 there was a buzz on the streets about a gay cancer. I lived a few blocks from the Castro neighborhood. The Castro was a fun bustling neighborhood of wall-to-wall men joyfully cruising, playfully flirting, and making sassy comments, delighting in the sexual freedom of being out in the open loving men.

I remember walking down Castro Street and there in the Star Pharmacy window was a large Department of Public Health (DPH) poster showing a white man's leg with a few roundish dark red splotches alerting the gay community to a new gay cancer, with a phone number to call and report the symptoms to DPH. There was very little information.

Nothing would ever be the same. The vibrant gay neighborhood scene shifted quickly. So many young men fell ill and died within a couple of weeks. Familiar neighborhood faces gaunt, purple blotches appearing, once muscle-toned bodies frail using a cane, jobs lost, inability to pay rent, nowhere to go. The illness forced many out of the closet. The fear, grief, and uncertainty was palpable. What caused it? Who's next? There were no real answers. A diagnosis was a death sentence. When someone was hospitalized there were no visitation rights for their lover and friends. They were not recognized as family. Many mortuaries refused the bodies. It was truly horrific, and the US government was doing nothing.

I started going to early STOP AIDS Project meetings and hearing people say they already knew 100 people who had died. It was hard to fathom, to make sense of it all. By then we knew body fluids including blood had something to do with transmission. The homophobic fundamentalist evangelical voices in the media came down hard—this was god's punishment.

The first person in my inner family circle who died of AIDS was my kids' fifth-grade schoolteacher, Gil Velasco. We came out to each other after I divorced. He was such a beloved teacher the flag flew at half-mast at his suburban school. This sort of recognition and respect was unheard of then, especially for an elementary school teacher. I stopped counting people when he died and wondered why I had been doing it. I remember the first time I kissed a person with HIV/AIDS. He was an activist I knew. He was leaving for one of the first international AIDS conferences in Denmark or Amsterdam. It was one of those slow-motion moments. I kissed his cheek and gave him a long hug. I hated the ongoing fear of everyday intimacy. There was no test until 1985.

BiPOL Educate · Advocate · Agitate

Eventually Bill and I met five other out bisexual activists in the gay community. In March 1983 we formed BiPOL a feminist bisexual political action group founded to educate, advocate, and agitate. The seven of us were a smoke and mirrors operation. Each one of us was visible and active in different areas of the gay and lesbian communities and movement. We spoke out representing bisexuals and our community. We would come back to our meetings asking—Where are they? We were all familiar with the deep closet.

As the first feminist bisexual political action group we jumped into action setting up an educational picket line in front of the Haitian embassy. STOP ARRESTING GAY AND BISEXUAL MEN ~ Haiti's tourist industry was in ruins due to racist US health authorities linking and therefore blaming HIV/AIDS

Lani Kaʻahumanu, 1984 San Francisco Lesbian and Gay Pride Parade BiPOL contigent. Courtesy of Arlene Krantz.

on Haiti. To counter this, they were going into the bars and randomly arresting gay and bisexual patrons.

The HIV/AIDS crisis affected all our lives. Gay and bisexual men continued to fall ill. Our communities rose up with a justifiable and uncontainable rage ACT UP/FIGHT BACK, SILENCE = DEATH. AIDS educator and therapist Dr. David Lourea of BiPOL was appointed to Mayor Dianne Feinstein's first AIDS Commission. He challenged the ongoing insistence AIDS was a gay disease, everything including education was gay, gay, gay and bisexual men were contracting AIDS and dying too. Targeted prevention messages were not being developed for bisexuals because bisexuality was a stage, and not a legitimate sexual orientation. I knew gay men who were having sex with lesbians. I was challenging and working to educate organizations to include bisexual in the safer sex material they were developing especially for youth. Once I was told "we don't deal with tuna fish"—I was stunned and outraged by his misogyny.

Bisexual men quickly became the mainstream media's scapegoat for the spread of HIV/AIDS. As if a sexual identity alone rather than behavior could spread the virus. David worked with the Department of Public Health to include bisexual men in the weekly statistics. Finally in 1984 after two years the SF DPH included bisexual men in their official statistics. This acknowledgment set the standard for health departments nationwide which had only recognized gay men. Unfortunately, bisexuals are still erased and scapegoated to this day. Others of us in

BiPOL went to the bathhouses, the S&M and sex clubs to do safer sex education. We spoke up for women with HIV/AIDS and sex workers of all genders. We worked to develop and teach safer sex protocols and were involved with a long-range women and AIDS research study. API artist and activist Lenore Chinn started an ongoing Lesbian Blood Drive in the Castro.

As the death toll rose President Ronald Reagan remained silent. San Francisco mayor (now senator) Dianne Feinstein's AIDS budget was more than Reagan's AIDS budget for the entire country. Reagan's first public mention of AIDS was not until 1985, four years after it was identified. Thousands of people had already died. He didn't give an actual speech about AIDS until 1987, a few months before the end of his term.

Reading the obituaries in the *Bay Area Reporter*, a local gay newspaper, became a weekly grieving ritual. Photos with a short obituary were published on both sides of the centerfold section. So many were dying you couldn't keep up. This was the only way to find out who died and when and where the memorial services would be held.

Street Theater—Ka'ahumanu for Vice President of USA

Part of what kept me going and sane in a time of so much death and despair was political theater. The 1984 Democratic National Convention (DNC) was held at the Moscone Convention Center in San Francisco. The City provided two protest stages across the street. Can you imagine that?

Back in January, Alan Rockway had gone to City Hall and filled out the paperwork, paid the fee, and BiPOL was issued a two-hour permit for the stage. At our next meeting he told us about the permit and that there'd be 5,000 extra reporters in town. They'd arrive early and would be looking for stories, especially local color stories. Our goal was bisexual visibility. We had lots of time to figure out what we'd do on the stage. I could tell by the look on his face he had a plan. But when he said he'd registered me, Lani, to run as BiPOL's vice-presidential candidate at the convention my head was spinning. "What a story," he said "Lani Ka'ahumanu will be the first out bisexual Hawaiian to run for Vice President of the United States." He explained any candidate who registers to run for this office has to collect 200 delegate signatures, even the presidential candidate's VP choice. Those who secure 200 signatures are given 15 minutes on the convention floor to nominate their candidate. You can use this time any way you want! Free media was invaluable. At the time television had three main TV channels, all carried the entire convention live.

We kicked off my run for VP with a press release announcing a BiPOL press conference at 1 p.m. in front of Moscone Convention Center introducing Lani Kaʻahumanu, our vice-presidential candidate and our platform. I was a nervous wreck. Six big-city reporters including Chicago, Miami and Los Angeles showed up to interview BiPOL's candidate. The next day a two-inch story appeared in the *SF Examiner*. We entered the local color arena.

BiPOL also staged a sexual healing of anti-gay fundamentalist Reverend Jerry Falwell, who was in town doing a Brotherhood Family Forum. We had a boombox blaring the song "I am what I am" from the gay Broadway musical *La Cage aux Folles* and sprinkled fairy dust glitter on the sidewalk outside the Forum's hotel and held signs protesting his homophobic 1984 Falwellian Agenda. This also garnered a little local story in the press.

It was a busy time. We put on our purple Kaʻahumanu for VP T-shirts and began the work of gathering delegate signatures. The easiest was attending a few of the 51+ delegate parties held at various hotels. They were open to the public and over-the-top extravagant—open bars with specialty drinks and incredible food representing the area like Texas BBQ and tequila drinks. It was wild and fun. We ate and collected signatures from many tipsy delegates telling them we wanted 15 minutes on the floor. They didn't care one way or the other; it was party time. There was a solar energy activist running for VP and collecting signatures too. For good measure we collected 253 signatures. We delivered the signatures to the DNC headquarters at the appointed time and waited.

In the end they told us we had too many alternate delegate signatures and canceled over 35 percent of our signatures. We marched up to DNC headquarters on the fourth floor of the Hilton Hotel. Everyone was at the convention center except two young volunteers. We told them what had happened, and that we were going to check the signatures. Amazingly we found the binders and signatures. They left to get security. Before the cops arrived, we'd found many of our rejected so-called alternate signatures were delegates. Clearly the DNC didn't want us on the convention floor addressing the lack of HIV/AIDS funding, demanding more research, and speaking up for GLB families, anti-nuclear proliferation, and passing the Equal Rights Amendment.

The First Bisexual Rights Rally

The day after our hoped-for 15 minutes on the floor was dashed and presidential nominee Walter Mondale chose Geraldine Ferraro to run as his vice president, we put the final touches on the first bisexual rights rally held on the protest stage across the street from the Moscone Convention Center. There were 13+ speakers, performances, the Sisters of Perpetual Indulgence, and a Ronald Reagan impersonator who was booked in a downtown comedy club and heard about the bisexual rally and asked if he could join us and perform! Sometimes there were more people on and behind the stage than in the audience. Everyone there knew we were making history.

1987 March on Washington for Lesbian and Gay Rights

In 1987 a second National March on Washington for Lesbian and Gay Rights was called. The Supreme Court *Bowers v. Hardwick* decision outraged the community. The Supreme Court upheld the constitutionality of a Georgia sodomy law criminalizing oral and anal sex in private between consenting adults, in this case homosexual sodomy. A huge civil disobedience action was planned on the steps of the Supreme Court. My article "The Bisexual Movement—Are We Visible Yet?" was in the official Civil Disobedience Handbook.[2] This was the first article on the bisexual movement to appear in a national gay and lesbian publication.

A national bisexual contingent was organized. Two women from the Boston Bisexual Women's Network contacted Autumn Courtney and me asking if BiPOL's Post Office Box could be used for their flyer "ARE YOU READY FOR A NATIONAL BISEXUAL NETWORK?" We agreed to handle the response. There was a pre-march contingent gathering. The stack of flyers disappeared quickly. The response to the flyer was overwhelmingly positive; people were excited. BiPOL and the Bay Area Bisexual Network (BABN) decided to host the first National Bisexual Conference in 1990. One workshop track was dedicated to national network organizing. There were 464 attendees, from 5 countries and 20 states. BiNET USA was born out of the initial labors of that conference. I was one of 6 national coordinators elected at the meeting in Minneapolis/St. Paul.

Bi Any Other Name

In 1991 Loraine Hutchins and I co-edited the groundbreaking feminist anthology *BI ANY OTHER NAME Bisexual People Speak Out* (Alyson Publications).[3]

---

2. Lani Ka'ahumanu, "The Bisexual Movement—Are We Visible Yet?" in *Out & Outraged: Non-Violent Civil Disobedience at the U.S. Supreme Court. For Love, Life & Liberation, Civil Disobedience Handbook*, 47–48, https://nonviolence.rutgers.edu/item/112 (accessed November 22, 2023).
3. Loraine Hutchins and Lani Ka'ahumanu, eds., *Bi Any Other Name: Bisexual People Speak Out*, 1st ed. (Boston: Alyson Publications, 1991).

This was the book Loraine and I needed when we came out. There are 76 coming-out stories, including our own. Mine is titled "Hapa Haole Wahine." The book was flying off the shelves. *Bi Any Other Name* rode the crest of the wave of the grassroots bisexual community and national bisexual movement organizing. Our book broke the silence, and empowered everyday bisexual people, activists, organizers, and our allies, too, to speak out. Our book was listed on the Lambda Literary Top 100 GLBT Books of the 20th Century, and in 2007 a Mandarin translation was published in Taiwan. There is an Italian translation in the works now.

1993 March on Washington

Change was afoot. In August 1991 Loraine and I got a call from API activist Glenn Magpantay, co-chair of the National Lesbian, Gay, and Bisexual Student Caucus of the United States Student Association. He'd just attended the first meeting for a 1993 March on Washington and there were no out bisexuals present. He told us the next meeting was going to be in Los Angeles.

My immediate gut reaction was the time was ripe to have bisexual in the title of the next March on Washington. Bisexuals have the infrastructure, the grassroots networks, and most importantly out bisexual activists and organizers in most major cities were working with gay and lesbian people, organizations, elected officials, and leaders. They'd served on committees, produced and tabled at events, marched, and were an integral part of their communities. Lesbian and gay leaders and organizations had been talking the talk but had never really been asked to walk the walk as far as publicly supporting bisexual people.

I wrote a statement endorsing bisexual inclusion and organized a twelve-city campaign for bisexual activists to collect signatures of support from their local and regional lesbian and gay community, cultural and movement leaders. I also understood this would be a visible next step for those individuals involved in asking for signatures and a timely coalescing of the grassroots and national bisexual movement. Yes, all this was accomplished on a landline phone and an answering machine! Over 50 signatures of prominent leaders were collected. BiPOL and local bisexual activists arrived early for the January1992 Name-the-March meeting in LA. We volunteered to collate and stuff the national meeting's attendee folders for the next morning's meeting. Copies of the signed endorsement were placed inside and on top of the flyers.

I also served on the San Francisco Bay Area MOW Steering Committee and was a Northern California representative. We were pushing for transgender and bisexual inclusion in the title and worked with a couple other states who also wanted bisexual and transgender in the title. When we arrived, we strategized with Jazz and Princess from Seattle, the only out transgender representatives. We began to lobby for the inclusion of transgender and bisexual. We worked the crowd before the meeting during breakfast, during the breaks, and at the evening social event. But a majority of people had no information, education or contact with transgender people in their communities. The inclusion of transgender people was voted down. There were many issues with adding bisexual too. In the end it got down to bisexual was too sexual. Many state representatives, especially from the more rural states "couldn't go back home with sexual in the march title." I understood AND isn't sexual liberation what this is all about, how it all began? Anyway, it finally came down to the Bisexual Caucus agreeing to drop sexual so that's how the title became the National March on Washington for Lesbian, Gay and Bi Equal Rights and Liberation.

I was honored to be one of 18 speakers chosen to address the crowd from the main afternoon stage. There were no out transgender speakers on that stage. I was the lone out bisexual and predictably I was given the eighteenth slot. The stage was almost an hour behind schedule due to the many impromptu appearances of Hollywood stars, politicians, and sports figures. The park service was threatening to turn off the sound. The time limits on the stage permits had passed the time allowed. Scout, one of the four co-chairs, asked me to cut my five-minute speech in half. I was angry and immediately turned to my backstage support team, Loraine, Katharin, and my daughter Dannielle. Nadine, another co-chair, came over to find out what happened. When I told her she said, "Oh no that's wrong," and left to see what she could do and in the very next moment I was told to go to the stage to speak. It was up two flights of stairs. CSPAN and documentarian cameras were rolling but the media tents had already been dismantled and the reporters doing post-speech interviews were gone.[4] The production crew was breaking down the stage and there I was being introduced—I stepped up and said, "Aloha, it ain't over till the bisexual speaks."

All pau.

---

4. User Clip: Lani Kaʻahumanu, 1993 March on Washington, https://www.c-span.org/video/?c4792729/user-clip-lani-kaahumanu-1993-march-washington (accessed November 22, 2023).

10

Keoni Ka'apuni
Creating the Self

I go by the name Keoni Ka'apuni. My legal name is Gregory Oliver. I was born and raised in Wai'anae and when I was a kid I moved to Makakilo and then Hālawa Heights. I spent the weekends with my grandparents in 'Ewa. My grandfather was a paniolo, he would ranch. Every weekend and in the summers I would live with them 'cause in the Hawaiian tradition, the oldest son usually went with the grandparents. They would hānai the oldest son and raise them. My dad was very modern and was like, "no!" But, they had us on the weekends, my brother and I were close in age, so I went too. It was a Hawaiian family so it was all the same to me, it was the country, nobody was rich, it was all the same. This changed when we moved to Makakilo and Hālawa Heights, we were around fewer Hawaiians, more Asian people and haole people like that.

I was the second oldest of five. Originally, my grandparents on my mom's side are from Big Island and Moloka'i. My uncle and a lot of them live on Moloka'i still. My dad's side, I don't know. They came from the Philippines. My grandma worked for the military, she was civilian but worked for the military. During the Second World War she was in charge of all the laundry and she was the personal seamstress for the general that ran the Navy. I have no idea what my grandfather did for a living. I wasn't really close with them.

I was baptized Catholic, but I have a real disdain for that. I had a natural compulsion towards that. I didn't understand it, didn't like it. Everything I knew about Hawaiian culture, I liked and understood. My culture, my 'aumakua, all of that stuff, I completely related to and got it. The God thing was so strange to me!

Boys and Girls Things

My dad was in the military, but not during Vietnam. I think it was winding down when I was a kid. When we were little, we went to the beach all the time. My dad was very outdoorsy and my grandpa was a paniolo so we were always outside. I had my own horse, I worked on the ranch with him sometimes. Go fish, throw net, all that classic old Hawaiian stuff. We would go to the mountains and pick guava, go hunting. My dad hunted pig, me and my brother went everywhere with him. We did all the stuff boys do with their dads. My dad was a boxer, so we boxed, which I loved doing. I loved the skill and artistry of it, but I wasn't into beating up people. It wasn't really a big deal for me. I wasn't really a competitive kid. I did a lot of sports, I loved it, but I didn't want to compete. The whole machismo attitude, it didn't really fit my personality. I identify as a māhū more than anything else now, so I can understand why I was like that then. When I reflect back, I understand now.

I always wanted to do other things, like I loved helping my mom, my grandmother, and doing anything with the girls. I could do both. It was very frustrating for my dad because I was so good at all the boys' stuff, but I was always interested in the girls' stuff and I was good at it. I would be doing both all the time. He would get really frustrated: "Why doesn't he like this? He's so good at this, but he's always doing girl stuff." I was always painting, creating stuff, music and eventually it became my career. He wanted me to be a boxer, but I was like nah, I can't do that. Beat up people for a living wasn't my thing.

When I was young, Hawaiian people were trained to look at māhū as a bad thing. When I heard the word, I knew it was a negative thing. I knew it was bad, but for me it didn't feel bad. It's something about that word, I think it's just because I felt connected to it in some way. I couldn't explain it, because you're a child and can't really articulate what you're feeling but I was like, I don't think that word is that bad. As I got older, as I learned more and I experienced the world more, I was like, "Yeah I am māhū, that's right baby!" Full on and now it's like can't stop it. It's changing I think, people now, heads are turning around and starting to realize it wasn't a bad thing. It was actually a really positive thing, part of our culture.

I was a really sheltered child. I was so self-absorbed in my art, my drawing, my life world. I spent a lot of time by myself, making up stories, writing, drawing, creating things, I was really introverted. I'm still introverted. When I'm not introverted is when I'm working, but when I'm not working, I very much don't want to talk to people, I just want to be by myself, my family, my husband, kind of private.

Campbell High School

I hated high school, but the thing is, I was a really great student when I was younger. I loved school until I had this traumatic experience with a teacher that physically abused me in front of everybody. That trauma changed me to hate school. I didn't like teachers and I didn't like authority. It was this horrible experience.

I remember the name was Mrs. Ruth, this haole woman and she was such a horrible racist. This was at Makakilo. It was a horrible experience and it just got worse. Up until then, I was a straight-A student. After that, I became the troublemaker, I would argue with the teachers, I was really anti-establishment. I was a little activist. Ohhh, I got in lots of trouble. Not like crime trouble. Luckily, I was akamai, I was a very smart kid, so I also read everything and I paid attention a lot. I would argue all the time with the principal, the teacher, and I almost got expelled twice. I would tell them the things they were doing were wrong. My mom supported me and my dad was like ugh. My mom knew I was right. Luckily my parents supported me with everything.

I started sports in the beginning, but I stopped. I was on the track and field team first, which I loved but then, the whole competitive thing again. Especially with your own team, so I stopped doing sports in school and I would do sports outside of school. I would do martial arts and swimming and eventually stopped that because the kids were so competitive and aggressive and I wasn't interested. I wanted to have fun. I was good, but it didn't appeal to me to be competitive. So, I only played in the beginning, by the time I was a junior, I didn't play sports at all.

I don't know what other teens were doing, maybe getting pregnant and smoking marijuana. It was Campbell High School, so it was a violent school. Every year Campbell and Wai'anae were in competition for most violent school. They were kind of like proud of it. There were always fights, but I never got into any. I was lucky because my brother was in high school with me and everybody was terrified. They knew we could box and my brother terrified people, he could kill you. So, I never had problems like that. I mean, I would have people calling me names and stuff like that, but I was so clueless, if someone called me a name I wouldn't even know. I was focusing on something else. People would tell me, "Hey that guy is calling you a māhū," and I was like, so what? I was like so clueless about that, it was not even on my radar. I was focused on other things.

I was such a weird kid. I studied classical voice when I was in high school. Our choir teacher, she was the first Samoan woman to ever go to Julliard. She sang opera and when I found out, I told her that I really wanted to take voice from her. This was in Hawai'i, at Campbell, so weird, right? At James Campbell, I would be singing an aria. In Hawai'i that kind of singing is very unusual. I was also doing theater too, so I was very occupied outside of school. I barely finished high school. I was a straight-D student, so bad. But I finished, I told myself I had to because I didn't want to have to repeat it. I had to get outta there, I didn't want to do another year.

Passion Dancers

I studied dance here, I studied with Nolan Goodman, who was a ballet teacher here. I also studied with James Dell and Mercello, who teaches at one of the high schools, I danced with him. And Simmion Dan, I would come and teach at their class, I would play music, I would teach at their studios. I started my dance pretty old, 13 or 14, and I paid for it myself 'cause my parents wouldn't pay for it. When I did a movie, I made all this money, so I was able to pay for my dance. After that when I was taking class, I never paid because I was given scholarships for it.

My parents were "Okay, next year" parents. They would always say they would pay next year, but they never did. You get used to this idea of things, people not coming through. When your parents don't come through as a child, you grow up thinking nothing is going to happen. You get used to the pattern of behavior, you kind of expect things to fall through. So, I had to pay for this myself. I got in a movie and I bought dance classes. They were furious. But I gave them half my pay and the other half I got dance classes. They couldn't argue with me. They got their cut! Pay the bills. I basically funded all my work and my whole career by myself. I did stuff at what is Diamond Head Theater now, by KCC. Shows at Chaminade, at UH. I did a musical at UH and then I left. They were doing a production of *Man of La Mancha*. I did stuff for Windward Community College and stuff like that, it was great. I was known around town. I would get a phone call and show up. I didn't go to the school.

The first regular paying job I got outside of the dance show was at the Jazz Cellar. I also used to work at Silly's. It was a disco, but I was in the male review, stripping for women, like Chippendales. I was the youngest teenage boy and all the other guys were all men, but all the ladies were like, cougars. I was like for the cougars. I would come out and they're all, "oooohhhhhh." So, I did that for the longest until I left, I was a stripper. So crazy that I did that for a long time. Some of the strippers were gay, some weren't, some were gay for pay. This one guy was supposedly straight. These two guys that were supposedly straight, I walk in and they were having sex in the dressing room. I was like, that's not straight! But honestly, I didn't really care, whatever people were I would just support.

I was never really out because I was never in. I just did my thing. I didn't identify as a gay person. I was just me. At that time, I did not have serious relationships. I was in love with a lot of people but I was so naive that I didn't know how. I had my first boyfriend in high school but that wasn't a relationship. It was more like him manipulating and taking advantage of me, he was a horrible person, horrible. And I was never in a relationship and he knew that I was māhū, he knew that I was gay, so he would manipulate me. He was a foster child going from home to home to home, so was really used to hustling people and getting stuff out of him and so he could smell how nice I was and he took advantage of me and it was horrible.

At 17 I had my own dance company called Passion Dancers. I was working for another dance company, a modern dance company doing little gigs around Waikīkī, little thing here and there. I was doing musicals, shows, singing in bands, I was getting a reputation in town, as a young kid that performs. I was at a club and some guy came up and asked if I was interested in doing a show in a nightclub. I said I could do a dance review, so at one point in the night they would cue up the dance floor and all of us would come out and do all of these dance routines. It was really cool. We would do it at the Hyatt, there was this club called Spats. It was like a disco. You went downstairs. I think there is a Chinese restaurant there now. It was really crazy and fun. I did that for a while, I also did a movie, a television show and made some money. I bought a ticket for New York and I left. Actually, I bought a ticket for my best friend because we were going to move together, but I didn't have any money for my ticket, so I entered a dance contest and the prize was a trip to New York and I won. That's how I got to New York.

Surviving in NYC

I was homeless because the place I was supposed to stay neglected to tell me I couldn't stay there because it was a co-op and only the owners could stay in the building. They knew I was coming months in advance. So, I was literally in the streets in New York City in the middle of winter. I had never seen snow. The first years, I go there in '82, I was sleeping on the streets. Sometimes I could find a place, but most of the time I was homeless. I was working at a gay bar as a waiter. Back then it wasn't as expensive as now, but for somebody on the streets it was and I couldn't find an apartment because I wasn't white. I would walk up to an open house and they wouldn't even hand me an application. They would just tell me I couldn't afford the place.

My first job was at a gay bar so the transition was easy. My best friend flew there first, got a job there and he convinced them to hire me before I got there. My best friend was this pretty white boy, blond hair, blue eyes. They thought I was going to be like him, another pretty white boy. When I came in, I am not that. The owner was this guy named Louis Katz, and he was this Jewish guy, old gay. He was crazy, very racist, but the manager still hired me. Everybody that works there was white, there were a couple Hispanic-looking guys but they all passed as white, and they spoke really good English. When they were at work, they were very proper. Anyway, he gave me the job.

I was there working for a couple months and the owner comes in. He would come in once in a while, but I was never working. One day he comes in and I was there. The owner saw me and was like, "what's that?" He asked, "who's that?" He was told I worked there and he goes, "fire him." The manager tells me they're going to have to let me go. I asked why and they explained the owner doesn't want me there. I asked why and they told me why. I said, "that's really racist," and I had never lost a job for the color of my skin, so I got really angry. In that moment, he walked by and I attacked him, grabbed him by the throat and shoved him against the wall. I said, "You got a fuckin problem with me?" Then he looked at me and smiles and said, "I like you, you can stay." Well fast-forward a couple months and Louis Katz was gone, no one knows where he is. Then the FBI comes in, they were looking for him. He was a serial killer. Killed all his boyfriends, murdered all of them, four guys. He ran away, they eventually caught him in Brazil and he was living as a woman. He changed to hide from the authorities. He was on the show *America's Most Wanted*. He was a serial killer, that's why he like me because he was nuts! He was a serial killer! Isn't that crazy?

I was living on the streets most of this time, didn't really get a place until the '90s. I had places to stay sometimes like my best friend would have a new boyfriend and he would say I could stay with them. I would do that for two months then I would go somewhere else, then back on the street. It was very like that back then, I didn't think of myself as homeless. First of all, there wasn't that word, no one used that word "homeless," that word came around in the '90s. In the '80s, no one said the word "homeless" you know?

I was just jumping around from one place, sleeping on rooftops of buildings, at piers, in the car. I would stay up all night and I would sleep during the day because it was safer. I would go to the park and sleep on a park bench in New York. Then I would go to work and use the bathrooms and also, I would go to the gym because I joined the gym and I would use the showers at the gym. You couldn't tell that I was homeless because I took care of myself. All my stuff was at work in my locker, so I was living out of my locker and nobody knew because it was really kind of degrading, embarrassing.

So, I was having lunch with my best friend and he asked where I was staying or living and there was a slight hesitation in the question. For some reason I just told him I slept at the park last night. He freaked out and after we ate, I slept over his house that night and the next morning we walked to the bank. He went to the bank and he took out all his savings and gave me all this money. Two days later I had an apartment.

I found a friend of mine, her boyfriend needed an apartment so we got together we rented this apartment. It was very shady, the landlord was shady. It was all cash. Two months later I was homeless again because my roommate's boyfriend was a junkie, a heroin addict. He spent all the money one day while I was at work. I was homeless again for another couple of years. Then another friend found me, saw me on the streets. He asked me, "Where are you going?" and I told him and he was like, come with me. I moved in with him and stayed with him for like years. I slept on the floor.

The apartment was so small that all we had was a mattress and a sink. It was a room you had to share a shower and bathroom in the hall. I slept on the floor and he slept on a single mattress and it was the happiest time of my life. Me and my friend Lesley, we were really close, we had so much fun. It was just incredibly joyous and fun. It was beautiful, it was such a great time in my life. Then I was never homeless after that because then I had money. I started working a lot so I started saving some money and then my hānai brother was in New York so I moved in with him at his spot after that. But that was almost ten years of homelessness.

AIDS & Activism in NYC

In New York it became very kind of, almost you had to kind of like say what you are so you can find your tribe. So, I felt very like disassociated from the gay community because I found them to be incredibly racist. First of all, the gay community is incredibly racist and that's just the white cis in general. And not that many people know anything about Hawai'i, most people don't know about Hawai'i they don't know about Hawaiians. You get that really ignorant kind of pre-designed image that people assume when you're Hawaiian. It was strange so I was kind of always like my own person. But because of what was happening with AIDS in New York I had to get involved in all of it.

I would travel around the country with Elizabeth Taylor, amfAR (the American Foundation for AIDS Research), raise a lot of money with them. I did a lot of activist work, very much involved in that stuff. Did benefits, you kind of had to. If you didn't you would just be like sitting around waiting to die. You like kind of had to get active. You just sat around, you're just waiting to die. You might as well be active so you feel like you can be of service then you can get your mind off of it. A lot of people died. The first person that I knew that died was my manager at my job, when I was working at the bar. Before my career took off, I was still working at the bar, as a waiter. In one week, the manager was there and the next week he was dead. In one week! That's how fast we were dying. It was crazy and it lasted for so long. It eventually slowed down but it got worse and worse and worse. It was really, really bad. It was scary too because you're like worried you're going to catch it, so it was very hard.

AIDS was worse than COVID when it came to stigma. COVID is bad, you can get it through breathing, whereas AIDS was through blood, so it could be through drug use or sex. The stigma of AIDS was unbelievably hard. You saw the evil in people, how people hate. COVID wasn't like that with stigma. I mean you see how polarizing it is and how ridiculous it is in this country. It is actually amazing how they have been able to use it as a tool to attack minorities and disenfranchised people. We know the wealthy get the better treatment, that has always been the case in this country. AIDS was really difficult because you would get so much hatred because you are queer because of AIDS. If you traveled it was horrible. There were people who didn't want to come around and stuff like that so it was really bad.

I wasn't in any serious relationships. Also, I was smart because I practiced safe sex. I wasn't going crazy but because of the diseases I was paranoid. Turns out

Keoni Ka'apuni. Courtesy of Jesse Winter.

this was good. I look back and I'm like it was smart to be paranoid because it kept me alive. Whereas a lot of my friends did not survive, it was a scary, scary time.

Raven O

I was called all kinds of things. The first time I was ever called the n-word was in a cab. I was thinking, oh people think I'm Black? I did a show once and the *New York Times* wrote a review and they called me a "tall, wily, Black man," and I thought it was hilarious. I got mislabeled a lot. I would go to auditions and they would never know what I was. When they asked, I would tell them that I was Hawaiian. They would be like, no. I wouldn't get the job. I just started producing my own shows. I would produce my own show because I kept getting called back and at the final call back, I wouldn't get it. They would always give it to the same. If you looked at the people, it was always the same, there's like eight white guys, one Black guy, and maybe an Asian, and then maybe me. The only people that would get cast was the white. It was ridiculous. I never got cast, but they kept calling me back. I finally got into a show, a Broadway show and it was very exciting. I called my parents and was like so excited. I was there for a year and got into a Broadway show and then a week after they called me and told me they changed their minds. They said I wasn't ethnic looking. Like, what?

It was the original company on Broadway for *La Cage Aux Folles,* the very first time they did it. After a year they give a replacement company and they do a touring company and it was the first replacement company that I auditioned for and got a pass but then they changed their mind and asked somebody else to be a part of it. After that I stopped, that's when I stopped auditioning for things. I stopped going out for anything that was commercial or status quo and I just decided to produce my own shows. Just like here. I would produce my own show and direct my own show. Eventually down the line, studios would come to me and offer me jobs and I didn't have to audition. If you asked me to audition, I would say no. I would say if you want me then you can just hire me because I'm not auditioning. And then they would hire me! They would say, okay. Obviously, you want me, you are calling me, so hire me. If you're not sure, then don't hire me. But it was rough!

I started making quite a lot of money. I mean, I own my home here, I own my home in New York. It was great, you know also when you get to that point, you learn how to do business, so you know your value. I wasn't greedy, but I was willing to walk away from a job. My own show was basically me and my musicians kind of like doing songs, telling stories, all very like autobiographical stuff. But I was touring with other shows that I was directing and performing, they were multimedia, circus, cabaret-type Cirque de Soleil type shows. I was in Cirque de

Soleil for like three years. I would do a show with them for a long time. I did that in Vegas and *Zumanity*. I worked with them again for another show. This amazing company hired me to be the lead in the show they were producing and I helped write the show for them. I did that for like three years and then I opened two venues, one in New York and one in London that is still open called the Box. So, yeah it was work work work.

I just did a gig in Mānoa last week. They were so happy they just asked if I would consider doing four nights. It all depends on my condition, if I can do it, I would do two nights. My body can't do four nights. I can't do it anymore, I used to work seven nights a week. Now I'm like, I think I can do two. But even that one show, physically it was a lot of work. I don't think I can do four, not anymore. It's kind of sad, but I'm supposed to be retired. I told them they have to pay me cash because I don't want to claim this shit. I'm like applying for disability and if they found out I would get screwed.

Becoming Māhū

For a while I thought I was a trans woman, so for years, I was living as a woman with my two friends who are trans women. That was an amazing time, that's when I really started coming into my own as far as realizing who I was and really embracing who I was being gay. It's my identity, I started realizing, oh I'm māhū and that's when it became very real. And as soon as that happened, I was like, "ahhhhh" this is perfect. But it was really an intense time. Luckily, I had two trans sisters who were really, really, intelligent and educated and really powerful. It was a really amazing time in my life.

The most amazing time of my life was when I was living as a trans woman as opposed to now. Now is incredibly obvious but back then it was kind of this intense, everything is under a microscope when you're trans, everyone is looking at you and judging you. Everybody! Gay people, straight people, every single person 'cause you're like this, this strange creature, right? Nobody understands, and nobody accepts, and everybody, like literally I mean it, we don't understand. I mean, we understand that kind of racism, and being women, we know misogynists and stuff like that. But, to be a trans woman of color, I mean you talk about hate, it's coming from everywhere, gay people, from women, from this color, this, that, everybody. Then you have your own self-loathing, it's just intense. But at the same time, because I had two incredibly powerful trans women with me, you know they made me. We were all very close and they are incredible women. One became a veterinarian, in the country up in Connecticut, taking care of horses and animals. The other one is a very successful, famous, retired supermodel and artist.

Eventually I came to the conclusion that I am māhū. In my own knowledge and my own culture, just being aware. When I was growing up there was no like Hawaiiana, they didn't teach that. And there's no internet, so I had to do everything on my own. So, there is a lot of false information, you know especially living in New York you can't find anything, so I had to really work hard. They didn't even teach Hawaiian, I'm only now learning. My grandparents didn't teach us it, you know they were brainwashed, stigmatized to not teach the young.

You know when my grandparents were young, the Queen, Queen Lili'uokalani was still the Queen, so they had to experience that takeover and that depression and that horrible being treated, you know in losing everything. So, they had to experience that and it traumatized them and it's totally generational. My grandpa told my mom, "do not marry a Hawaiian, stay away from Hawaiians, only marry haole or Japanese." My mom of course married a Filipino. Although her first husband was Japanese but he didn't tell them that he was sterile. Because in the military he got injured and couldn't have kids. So, you know Hawaiians, if you cannot have kids, he was off.

So, months after they got married my mom divorced him and then met my dad; the second worst thing, Filipinos. My grandparents were not happy, "Not Filipino!" But that stigma was there, my grandparents didn't teach anything, it was very hard. They would teach us little things here and there, most of it was through observation, being around them as much as possible.

It was a very interesting time so for me, it was a no-brainer, māhū. And it took that experience of living as a trans woman. I realized I wasn't trans while going to the bathroom, I was going to the bathroom, I was making shishi, I was standing up, trans women don't stand up when they use the bathroom, I was like, oh, and I knew. I was like why am I standing up? Then I had a moment of clarity, "okay you're not trans, you're māhū, you're both." That's what I said to myself, and so you're māhū. So, I came out and told everybody, they were very disappointed. They almost felt like it was a betrayal because here we are the three of us. The three of us were very powerful because we did a lot of work together, we were like performers, the three of us, and I was kind of the bedrock, I was the one that directed the show, choreographed it, and I was the one who organized it, I was like the brains of everything. And then all of a sudden, I was not going to be doing that anymore. We had our own band, our little rock band, the three of us. I left. It was a trans band and I was no longer trans, so I left the band. It was really, really traumatic for them, but we're still very close friends.

Māhū is very much a two-spirit person, it's both, you know what I mean? If you know anyone who identifies as māhū, Kumu Hina is a great example of that you know, because she's obviously female but she's also not obviously male, but she acknowledges that. I don't know her but when I hear her speak, I watch her, she's just amazing. She's like a nice, very confident in who she is. So, for me, I'm more the other side of the spectrum, I look more male than I look female, but I still identify as both. Some trans women start thinking of themselves as just like a woman, like, "I am a woman" and I'm like, well, you're a trans woman, embrace that. You're the other gender, which is a beautiful thing and you should embrace that.

I keep telling younger trans kids to be your own woman, don't worry about those people, focus on yourself. That process is such a difficult process and they have go through that process on their own, come to their own conclusions, and I'm like it's nobody's business how you identify. It's just you support it and be kind, just support it and be understanding about it. If somebody tells me they're trans, if I don't know it, 'cause sometimes I'm so clueless like I can't tell anymore. If they say "oh I'm trans" automatically in my head I understand them better. 'Cause I understand what they went through 'cause I've gone through that. I've lived it, I understand it better. I've gone through the process of transition, but I'm not really a trans woman, I've gone through those experiences, all that stuff that goes on around it. I don't know internally what they go through because that's a biological, mental, spiritual journey they're on. But I understand a trans woman much more than I do a non-trans, cis woman. So, I look at those things very specifically. I don't treat everybody equally 'cause we are not the same. Everybody I treat equally but not the same. 'Cause everybody is an individual, they have their own story, experience, and journey so you have to learn about that. Like everybody has their own trauma. So sadly, a lot of people's trauma dictates how they move in the world, sadly, most people.

Coming Home

I only moved back because my husband wanted to live here. I wouldn't be here if it wasn't for him. I can't work because of my degenerative bone disease so I was forced to retire. Because of COVID I couldn't get treatment, so it kind of progressed so bad that I'm disabled now. It's really difficult, so I moved back home. I never really thought about coming back before. I liked traveling and seeing the world. I also like being the Hawaiian out in the world telling people I'm from Hawai'i and promoting Hawai'i and kind of being an ambassador of Hawai'i. I love that! Just telling people what Hawaiian is, I still do that a lot now. My older brother said you have to come home and heal and get better. He was right. I came home and got much better. Still not 100 percent, it's fine, it is what it is.

I thought Hawai'i was doing good but when I came back, I was like, what the fuck happened? I was like shocked at how bad it was, how corporate it was. I mean it was not as bad then as it is now. I'm fervently disappointed. I'm really disappointed at how fractured the Hawaiian movement has become, there are so many fractures. Haunani-Kay Trask was one of my heroes so I followed her when she was alive and when she would say, "I am not American . . . I'm Hawaiian," that's like duh right? And I would constantly tell people you have to break that colonial conditioning and it's very difficult. It's not serving you it's only serving them. It's been difficult, it's been hard to watch and digest.

I live in Waikīkī out of convenience, 'cause I don't drive. We don't like to drive and didn't want to live far away and drive everywhere. Also, he likes the Walls, so everything is about Walls you know. So, I was thinking live in Waikīkī and you can just walk to places, we don't do anything. I don't leave my house because I can't walk around too much because of my disability, I can't get around. I'm a beach person, I love the mountains though. All my 'ohana all live up in the mountains so I have to go and visit them all the time.

Now I'm just painting. I had an exhibition at Marks Garage, one of the art museums, um yeah, selling art. Sold another piece yesterday. I've been involved in the arts all my life and so I've met a lot of artists. I've always been a painter, I've designed every costume on every set, every prop in every show, that's a lot of sets, a lot of stuff. I been painting since I was a kid and I've had a few art exhibitions through my career, I just haven't gone full speed into it. It's hard to do two different things, so now it's kind of full-on with the art. I really can't do much, I can't really paint a lot, I have to paint then stop. I started painting today but then I realized I can only paint maybe an hour or two at a time, then I have to stop and rest. You know the show was great, but it was very difficult 'cause I can't take any painkillers while I'm doing the show, 'cause if I take painkillers I feel off, I can't sing, I can't dance, so I was in a lot of pain by the time . . . halfway through the show. Racking pain so it was really hard, that's why I'm like hmmmm I can do this maybe twice a week not four, make some extra money.

It is healing to come home to Hawai'i. As soon as I came here, I just felt like one hundred times better. Because when you live in New York you don't, there's no 'āina, there's no connection right. As soon as I came home it's just like everything aligned and everything was just fine. Other people they don't understand, also if they're haole they don't understand because they aren't from an Indigenous culture or tribal culture. Whenever I would come home to visit, I always felt fixed, like literally fixed. And when we first came back it was still COVID but you could still go to the ocean, so I was in the ocean every day but my back just got worse and then I went into treatment, treatment didn't work so I have another surgery next month, so we'll see what happens.

It's been good, it's been very healing, and also you know being around my people, my culture it's kind of like a breath of fresh air reconnecting, reevaluating everything and it's been a good thing. I still miss my old life 'cause I was traveling so much, until I have to get on a plane, I'm like I don't miss this. I went back to New York to do some work after COVID, that's when I realized I could not do it anymore, I thought I could still do it. Then just traveling, it was like oh my goodness I can't do this, it's too painful. So, I told my husband and he was happy 'cause he was done with me traveling, 'cause all I did was travel for work. So being home has been good.

Epilogue

The intial purpose of this project was to document the experiences of LGBTQM kupuna, to create space for their voices and acknowledge their contributions to LGBTQM and Hawaiian life. Their animated stories produced an archive of Hawaiian history I had not anticipated. Their vivid descriptions of what life was like for them as a Kanaka LGBTQM person during the Hawaiian renaissance, amidst the struggle for Hawaiian sovereignty or at the height of the fight for same-sex marriage, served as a reminder of how much emotional and physical labor was expended so that present-day Kānaka LGBTQM could imagine different possibilities for ourselves. The interviews were at times light and humorous to gloss over painful memories, while in other moments, their reflections were pointed critiques of the lāhui and of the non-Hawaiian LGBTQM community.

Several of the interviewees made declarations that "Hawaiians are super homophobic," which was surprising to hear out loud. The Hawaiian community in many ways believes itself as accepting, but the pendulum can always swing both ways. Every LBGTQM Kanaka person knows there is great variation of acceptance within the lāhui, although we rarely talk about it or we pretend we have collectively moved beyond it. The same homophobia and transphobia these kūpuna faced is intertwined with the current backlash against the LGBTQM community. We cannot forget that LGBTQM issues in Hawaiʻi are connected to the entire community. Legislative attacks on marriage equality and the right to health care for trans people is just the tip of the iceberg beneath which numerous examples of discrimination and microaggressions get played out in workspaces, homes, and playgrounds. With so much misinformation on social media, these issues are as urgent as ever. A recent study found that in Hawaiʻi, 1 in 10 youth identified as LGBTQM, nearly 5% of the adult population identifies as LGBTQM, and 30% are raising children.[1] According to a 2018 Gallup poll, Hawaiʻi had the largest

---

1. Hawaiʻi State Department of Health, *Hawaiʻi Sexual & Gender Minority Health Report*, 2017, https://health.hawaii.gov/surveillance/files/2017/05/HawaiiSexualandGenderMinorityHealthReport.pdf (accessed November 22, 2023).

proportion of transgender people (0.60%) in its population in the entire country. Notably, Hawai'i remains one of the few states where you can get an X as a gender marker on your driver's license or state ID and have gender-affirming health care covered by insurance.

Within the Hawaiian community, there's been an increase in the number of "out" Hawaiian LGBTQM celebrities and growing vocal support for LGBTQM issues by public officials. Since the start of this project, there was the Kapaemāhū exhibit at the Bishop Museum about the history of māhū and LGBTQM discrimination in Hawai'i, as well as two hana keaka (theater production), *Ho'oilina* and *Glitter in the Pa'akai,* both in 'ōlelo Hawai'i (Hawaiian language) with LGBTQM themes that premiered at the University of Hawai'i at Mānoa in recent years. The work of two activist māhū, Hinaleimoana Wong-Kalu and Dana Kaua'iiki Olores, were commemorated at Lā Ho'iho'i Ea (Hawaiian Independence Day) festivities in 2022, making it appear that within our Kanaka communities there is more awareness and acceptance than ever of LGBTQM people and relations. Hopefully this will continue to be the case, but it should also be remembered how precarious these changes or moves to inclusion are and how common it is for LGBTQM Kānaka at all ages to feel marginalized and devalued.

At every stage of life, we must make it possible for Kānaka to nurture whatever consensual connections and expressions we desire. As a lāhui we have to continue building and thinking of ways to support each other by creating opportunities to learn these histories and to amplify these voices. The lāhui benefits greatly from understanding this history. It is all of our kuleana to listen and remember that these voices do not need to compromise or choose between being Kanaka or LGBTQM. Instead, as these mo'olelo teach us, we are able to weave these parts of ourselves together and have it inform our lives in a way that is generative and fruitful. As several of the kūpuna expressed, being culturally grounded as Kānaka enabled many of them to survive and persevere. Let this collective mo'olelo be a commemoration of their struggle that is an integral part of our never-ending huaka'i as a lāhui navigating what it means to be Kanaka.

Bibliography

Advertiser Staff. "Kumu Hula, AIDS Activist Kahala Dies." *Honolulu Star Bulletin*, November 5, 1991.

Anbe, Brent, Jaymee Carvajal, Keali'i Reichel, and Kathryn Xian. *Ke Kulana He Māhū: Remembering a Sense of Place*. Honolulu: Zang Pictures, Inc., 2001.

Arista, Noelani. *The Kingdom and the Republic: Sovereign Hawai'i and the Early United States*. Philadelphia: University of Pennsylvania Press, 2018.

Bailey, Beth, and David Farber. *The First Strange Place: The Alchemy of Race and Sex in World War II Hawaii*. New York: Free Press, 1992.

Basham, Leilani. "Awaiaulu Ke Aloha: Hawaiian Sexuality, Gender, and Marriage." Unpublished manuscript, 2004.

Foucault, Michel. *The History of Sexuality*, edited by Frederic Gros, translated by Robert Hurley. 1st American ed. New York: Pantheon Books, 1978.

Goo, Melvin. "'Mahus Are People, Too'—Hawaii's Loneliest Citizens." *Honolulu Advertiser*, July 17, 1968.

Hall, Lisa Kahaleole Chang, and J. Kēhaulani Kauanui. "Same-Sex Sexuality in Pacific Literature." *Amerasia Journal* 20, no. 1 (1994): 75–82.

Hawai'i State Department of Health. *Hawai'i Sexual & Gender Minority Health Report*, 2017. https://health.hawaii.gov/surveillance/files/2017/05/HawaiiSexualandGenderMinorityHealthReport.pdf. Accessed November 22, 2023.

ho'omanawanui, ku'ualoha. *Voices of Fire: Reweaving the Literary Lei of Pele and Hi'iaka*. Minneapolis: University of Minnesota Press, 2014.

Hunter, Gene. "No Signs Point Way to 'Hangouts.'" *Honolulu Advertiser*, September 25, 1967.

Hutchins, Loraine, and Lani Ka'ahumanu, eds. *Bi Any Other Name: Bisexual People Speak Out*. 1st ed. Boston: Alyson Publications, 1991.

Jones, Bob. "Action Is Sought on Isle Deviants." *Honolulu Advertiser*, February 14, 1963.

Ka Lāhui Hawai'i. *Ka Lāhui Hawai'i, the Sovereign Nation of Hawai'i: A Compilation of Materials for Educational Workshops on Ka Lāhui Hawai'i*. Hilo: Ka Lāhui Hawai'i, 1993.

Ka Nupepa Kuokoa. Vol. IX, no. 40, October 1, 1870. "Ka Mo'olelo o Kamaakamahi'ai."

Ka'ahumanu, Lani. "The Bisexual Movement—Are We Visible Yet?" In *Out & Outraged: Non-Violent Civil Disobedience at the U.S. Supreme Court. For Love, Life & Liberation Civil Disobedience Handbook*, 47–48. https://nonviolence.rutgers.edu/item/112. Accessed November 22, 2023.

Kapaemāhū. Kanaka Pakipika & Pacific Islanders in Communications, 2020. http://www.kapaemahufilm.com/.

Kauanui, J. Kehaulani. *Paradoxes of Hawaiian Sovereignty: Land, Sex, and the Colonial Politics of State Nationalism*. Durham, NC: Duke University Press, 2018.

Merry, Sally Engle. *Colonizing Hawai'i: The Cultural Power of Law*. Princeton, NJ: Princeton University Press, 2020.

Osorio, Jamaica Heolimeleikalani. *Remembering Our Intimacies: Moʻolelo, Aloha ʻĀina, and Ea*. Minneapolis: University of Minnesota Press, 2021.

Pukuʻi, Mary Kawena.*ʻŌlelo Noʻeau: Hawaiian Proverbs & Poetical Sayings*. Bernice P. Bishop Museum Special Publication. Honolulu: Bishop Museum Press, 1983.

Rich, Adrienne Cecile. *Of Woman Born: Motherhood as Experience and Institution*. New York: W. W. Norton & Company, 1976.

Silva, Noenoe. "Pele, Hiʻiaka, and Haumea: Women and Power in Two Hawaiian Moʻolelo." *Pacific Studies* 30, no. 1–2 (2007): 159–182.

User Clip: Lani Kaʻahumanu, 1993 March on Washington. C-SPAN.org, n.d. https://www.c-span.org/video/?c4792729/user-clip-lani-kaahumanu-1993-march-washington. Accessed December 6, 2023.

"We Are Not American" speech. Haunani-Kay Trask—Speech from the Centennial of the Overthrow, ʻIolani Palace, January 17, 1993.

Young, Wes. "World of the Homosexual." *Honolulu Star-Bulletin,* February 29, 1964.

Index

Act 175 "Intent to Deceive" Law, 11
aikāne, 6, 27, 94, 95, 100, 113, 131
Akiu, Hōkūokalani, 3, 13, 14, 54
aloha: given or shared, 19, 39, 62; as intelligence, 97; spirit, 87, 97, 118
Aotearoa, 21, 22, 28, 39, 94, 96–98, 101, 102

bisexual, viii, 4, 6, 7, 11, 12, 31, 115, 123–128, 131; activism, 4, 125; movement, 129, 130

Catholic, 22, 31, 58, 79, 90, 121, 132
The Center (also known as the LGBT Community Center, the Gay Community Center, the LGBT Center), 30, 58, 59, 61, 63, 64
Chinatown, 10–12, 70, 71, 74, 109
Christian/Christianity, 2, 37, 47, 51, 57–59; ideals, 8; marriage, 1; missionaries, 7, 8, 102, 116
civil rights, 6, 8, 27
civil unions, viii, 15
class: middle class, 32, 120; social class, 9, 116; working class, 3, 20
clubs, 61, 62, 71, 75, 114, 127; the Blowhole Lounge, 71–74; the Clouds, 11, 72; Hulas, 105; the Gay 90s, 105; Midway Bar, 70; Sir John's, 70; Pōhaku's, 71; Pumehana Lounge, 71; Shindig Bar, 70
constitutional amendment, vii, 35
COVID-19, 29, 114, 115, 139, 143–145. *See also* pandemic

Defense of Marriage Act (DOMA), 14
drag queen, 71, 73, 76, 108

drag show, 84, 88
Dudoit, Nawahine, 3, 14, 24, 27, 39, 46

'Ewa/'Ewa Beach, 40, 64, 78, 132

Gabbard, Mike, 26, 27
gay marriage, 2 ,12, 14, 29, 50
the Glade (also known as "the Glades"), 4, 11, 73–76, 79, 80, 84, 85
Gomes, Kuʻumeaaloha, 2–4, 19, 24, 31, 32, 34, 36, 38, 45, 48, 59–61, 63, 101

haole/white: conflicts within LGBTQ community, ix, 25, 27, 32, 48; LGBTQ as "haole issue," ix, 25, 38, 60, 63
Haʻupu, Aunty Kim, 4, 78
Hawaiian renaissance, ix, 3, 69, 103, 106, 146
HIV/AIDS, xii, 12, 13, 42, 62, 76, 96, 107, 108, 124, 125–128, 138, 139
homophobia/homophobic, viii, ix, 13, 99, 100, 101, 125, 128; experiencing, 3, 146; within Hawaiian community, 14, 25, 32, 36, 37, 38, 95, 96, 146
hula: AIDS/HIV in hālau, 13, 62, 76; dancing and learning, 66, 68, 84, 103, 105, 106, 109, 110; māhū in hula, 95, 103, 105; men dancing, 57, 61, 68, 105
Human Rights Commission, 27

Ka Lāhui Hawaiʻi (sovereignty group), ix, 3, 8, 32, 38, 54, 58, 60, 63, 64, 66, 149
Kaʻahumanu, Lani, 4, 13, 115, 119, 120, 126–129, 131, 149, 150
Kaʻapuni, Keoni, 4, 13, 132, 139
Kahoʻolawe, 122

Kalihi, 54, 71, 72, 111
Kameʻeleihiwa, Lilikalā, 33, 60
Kamehameha Schools, xi, 43, 45, 54, 67, 68
Keaulana, Kimo Alama, 4, 11, 57, 58, 67, 69, 77
kumu hula, 13, 57, 61, 67, 106, 109, 110, 114, 117

lāhui, x, xi, 2, 8, 95, 146, 147
lesbian: community, 4, 12, 120, 121, 123; identity, 6, 7, 21–23, 42, 46, 89, 115, 124
LGBTQ political groups: ACT UP, 3, 108; Bay Area Bisexual Network (BABN), 129; BiNET USA, 129; BiPOL, 125, 127–130; STOP AIDS Project, 125
Lum, Bradford, 3, 13, 103, 104

māhū: as bad, 57, 63, 68, 78, 103, 133; community, 4, 78, 79, 80, 88, 115; history of, 2, 11, 12, 36, 37, 147; identity, 42, 49, 133, 134, 141, 142
mainland (also called "the continent"), 13, 84, 114; coming from, 14, 28, 48; coming home, 52, 56; living on, 4, 44, 115; moving to, 75
marriage equality, viii, 3, 14, 38, 59, 113, 146
Meyer, Manulani Aluli, 4, 89, 98
military, 20, 21, 80, 122, 132, 142; homophobia within, 10–12, 74; joining, 56, 68
Miller, Ken, 59
moe kolohe, 9

Nā Mamo o Hawaiʻi, x, 2, 3, 3n1, 14, 23, 44, 49, 50, 52, 53, 56, 59–61; changes within, 33, 60; legacy of, 29, 38; at the same-sex marriage hearings, 24, 27, 45; working in Hawaiian community, 28, 33, 63, 64
New York City, 4, 75, 136–138, 140–142, 144, 145

Pālolo, 3, 66
pandemic, 4, 5, 114
Prince Hanalei, 76
Protect Kahoʻolawe ʻOhana (PKO), 21

Puha, Kalei, 27, 29, 31, 45–52
Pūwalu, 25, 32, 33, 38, 51

race/racism, 14, 41, 138, 141
religion, 26, 113
Reserve Officers' Training Corp (ROTC), 54, 68

same-sex marriage: vii–ix, 12–15, 27–29, 63, 76, 77, 82; ban, 14; hearings, 2, 3, 23, 33; vote on constitutional amendment, 14, 28
San Francisco: activism, 24, 108, 126, 127, 130; living in, 3, 22, 103, 107–110, 118
"Save Traditional Marriage," vii
sexuality, viii–x, 5–7, 9, 12, 14, 23, 27, 36, 38
Silva, Noenoe, 3, 14, 24, 27, 31, 34, 57
sovereignty, viii–x, 3, 3n1, 6, 13, 14, 23, 25, 29, 31–33, 38, 56, 99, 146
sports, 41, 63, 91, 92, 105, 131, 133, 134
State Commission on Same-Sex Marriage, 2, 20, 24–26

tourism, 14
trans, 2, 94n1, 141–143; trans people, 30, 146, 147; transgender, 6, 7, 59, 63, 88, 130–131; transphobia, 146; transsexual, 88; transvestite, 4
Trask, Haunani-Kay, 14, 22, 36, 39n1, 144

University of Hawaiʻi: attending, 43, 53, 75, 91, 103, 105, 106; finding community, 2, 3n1; working at, 24, 29, 57, 62, 67
University of Hawaiʻi LGBT Center, 27, 30
University of Hawaiʻi LGBT Commission, 62, 64

vice squad, 4, 11

Waiʻanae, 4, 20, 54, 65, 78, 80–85, 87, 88, 132, 134,
Waikīkī, 12, 56, 60, 72, 73, 116, 117, 136, 144

Young, Jackie, 27

About the Editor

STEPHANIE NOHELANI TEVES (Kanaka Maoli) is an associate professor of Women, Gender, and Sexuality Studies at the University of Hawai'i at Mānoa, where she teaches courses on Indigenous feminisms and queer theory. Teves is author of *Defiant Indigeneity: The Politics of Hawaiian Performance* (University of North Carolina Press, 2018). She lives with her 'ohana in 'Ewa, Hawai'i.